THE HEART
IS FIRE

THE HEART
IS FIRE

The world of the
Cahuilla Indians
of southern California

Deborah Dozier

Heyday Books • Berkeley, California

Library of Congress Cataloging-in-Publication Data

Dozier, Deborah.
    The heart is fire. : the world of the Cahuilla Indians of southern California / Deborah Dozier.
        p.   cm.
    Includes bibliographical references (p. 155)
    ISBN 0-930588-89-4 (pbk.)
    1. Cahuilla Indians--Biography.   2. Cahuilla Indians--Interviews.
  3. Cahuilla philosophy.   I. Title.
  E99.C155D68 1998
  305.897'45--dc21   97-52347
                                                             CIP

Book design and cover art: Jeannine Gendar
Printing and binding: Dehart's Printing Services, Santa Clara, CA

Please address orders, inquiries, and correspondence to:
  Heyday Books
  P.O. Box 9145
  Berkeley, CA 94709
  (510) 549-3564, fax (510) 549-1889
  heyday@heydaybooks.com

Printed in the United States of America

10 9 8 7 6 5 4 3

To Mukat

for having the wisdom to give us elders

Grateful Acknowledgments

Cahuilla Voices: We Are Still Here and *The Heart is Fire* were possible only because of the valuable support of the following people and institutions. Their commitment and generosity celebrate cultural diversity in the most positive way. Their vision and understanding have created a permanent record of this view of modern Cahuilla culture. These supporters are engaging in future building of the highest order; they are building a future in which the best attributes of every culture contribute in a positive way to the quality of life for all those who share this planet.

Dolores (Dee) Alvarez
Cindi Alvitre
Eugene N. Anderson
Anthony Andreas
Paul Apodaca
Ron Baker
Lowell J. Bean
Pam Beck
Karen Bellinfante
Thomas Blackburn
Linda Bobo
Peter Bolz
Edna Bonacich
Pat Bottini
Phil Brigandi
Jim Brown
Scott Cairns
California Council for the Humanities
California Historical Society
Mike Capriotti
Barbara Carlson
Cannon Camera
Lori Sisquoc Cano
Ed Castillo
Duane Champagne
Maree Cheatham
Yue-Hong Chou
Steve Clugston
Craig Clyver
Brian Copenhaver
Carl Cranor
Susan Crawford
Kathleen Dafashy

Rick Danay
Becky Davis
Lee Davis
Lewis DeSoto
Lara Dozier
Sara Dozier
Hazel Duro
Georgia Elliott
Ron Engard
James Erickson
Joe Frazier
Vera Mae Fredrickson
Everet Frost
John Goodman
Jerry Gordon
Susan Gordon
Robert Griffin
Don Grinde
Jaclen M. Grove
Richard Haas
Stephen Hammond
Gloria Macias Harrison
Ken Hedges
Charlotte Heth
Robert Jackson
Terry Kondrack
Konklin Signs
Carolyn Kozo
Karen Kraut
Rebecca Kugel
Donna Largo
Harry Lawton
Mary Jane Lenz
Esther Levi

Robert Levi
Los Angeles Public Library
Special Collections
John Macarro
Malki Museum
Daniel McCarthy
Roy McJunkin
Robert McKimme
Sally McManus
Cathryn McNair
Bernd Magnus
Debbie Massey
JoMay Modesto
Mary Moore
Steve Morgan
Chris Moser
Vince Moses
Museum für
Völkerkunde, Berlin
Gladys Murphy
National Anthropologic Archives
National Endowment for the
Humanities
National Museum of the
American Indian
News from Native California
Virginia Ohr
Palm Springs Desert Museum
Palm Springs Historical Society
Terri Parsons
Peabody Museum of Ethnology
Patricia Perbetsky
Hannah Petzenbaum
Sherry Pope
Perpetua Press
Ramona Pageant
Carol Rector
Jeanne C. Reyes
Larry Reynolds
Riverside County Office of
Education
Riverside Municipal Museum
Riverside Public Library
Andrew Sanders
Katherine Saubel
Sherman Indian School Museum

Smithsonian Institution
Dianne Sieder
Alvino Siva
Cindi Smith
Southwest Museum
Karen Speed
Ines Talamantez
Dace Taube
Ron Tobey
Saturnino Torres
Cliff Trafzer
University of California
Humanities Research Institute
University of California,
Riverside:
California Museum
of Photography
Center for Ideas and Society
College of Humanities
and Social Science
Development Office
Food Service
Foundation Office
Grants and Contracts
Rivera Library
Special Collections
Media Resources
Publications & Reprographics
University Relations
University of Southern California
Special Collections
Rosalie Valencia
Sylvia Vane
Steve Walag
Katherine Warren
Faith Wilding
Paula Winter
Carole Zuloaga

Royalties and publisher's profits from sales of this book are contributed to a scholarship fund for reservation students administered by the Malki Museum. Contributions can be sent to: Malki Museum Scholarship Fund, Malki Museum, P.O. Box 578, Banning, CA, 92220.

CONTENTS

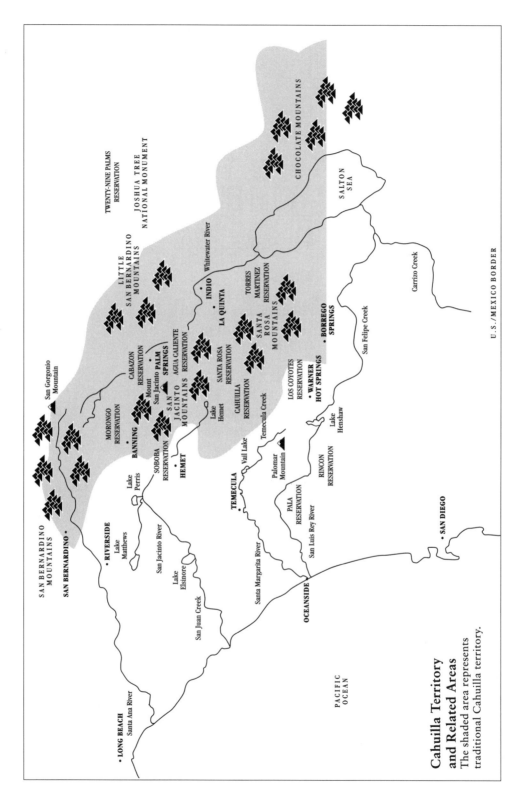

Cahuilla Territory and Related Areas
The shaded area represents traditional Cahuilla territory.

10

INTRODUCTION

THE CAHUILLA PEOPLE were created thousands of years ago by Mukat from the land which they consider their traditional home, a land that can be brutally hot or bitterly cold. The wind tears across the land, impeded only by the rocky, rugged, and extraordinarily beautiful mountains. It is a land of extreme contrast; palm trees shade the feet of snow-capped peaks, and raging torrents of melting snow course their way through shimmering sands.

This land is scarred by freeways and landfills, housing subdivisions and shopping centers, ranches and resorts, mines and military bases. This land is in a rapidly developing corner of southern California and has been overlaid with portions of San Diego, Riverside and Imperial counties. The Cahuilla are now confined to a few hundred thousand acres of federal reservation lands. Now they must ask permission to gather traditional foods and materials where others once asked their permission to trespass. It is a world turned upside down, no longer predictable, no longer ruled by the memories of the elders who were the linchpins of successful strategizing.

In prehistoric and historic times Cahuilla territory extended on the north to the San Bernardino Mountains, on the east to the middle of the Colorado Desert, on the south to the Santa Rosa Mountains and the area currently known as Borrego Springs, and on the west to the San Jacinto Mountains and parts of the San Jacinto and San Bernardino valleys. Over time, the Cahuilla had to adapt to physical environmental changes that changed the distributions of flora, fauna, and water. These changes were anticipated and expected. Although Cahuilla world view holds that all matter is likely to undergo unpredictable change, the forces precipitating the changes were well known. They were fire, flood, drought, cold, heat, wind, insect infestations, occasional illness, attack by marauding animals or people, and earthquake.

An understanding that the world was unstable allowed the Cahuilla to adapt. Village sites were temporarily or

> The Cahuilla were the first people who existed. They were here before this place became desert. They remember the mammoths who roamed the grassy plains eons ago. They went all around South and North America. Everywhere they went they left some people there. This is how people came to be in many places.
>
> —*Katherine Saubel*

11

permanently relocated and corresponding alterations in cropping and gathering patterns were made to cope with the inherent instability of the world. More recently, the confinement on reservations, land allotment systems imposed by outsiders eager to control the natural hot springs and other resources of the area, state and federal governments, and urban and suburban development of traditional Cahuilla lands have drastically changed the lifeways of the Cahuilla people.

Social patterns in prehistoric, historic, and modern Cahuilla culture are structured around the basic social units of moieties, sibs, and lineages. As Lowell Bean says in *Mukat's People,* "The Cahuilla kinship system is a very exact one which carefully distinguishes a large number of people and minimizes the number of people in one kin category."

As with many other native California groups, there are two Cahuilla moieties or marriage groups: the Wildcat and the Coyote. Wildcats and Coyotes were required to marry outside of their own moieties. In addition, prospective marriage partners of opposite moieties could not have a genealogical relationship traceable to within five generations. Moieties are comprised of subgroups known as sibs which function as political, economic, and ceremonial units, and are based on degree of common patrilineality. Each sib is further subdivided into three to ten lineages. Each lineage was an economically independent family unit with rights of ownership of essential stands of oaks, piñon, and mesquite. These groves were patrilinearly inherited.

Cahuilla social patterns have changed over time for a number of reasons. Marriages between children of enemy lineages could transform a relationship based on enmity and ridicule into one based on reciprocity. Wars occasionally wiped out entire lineages or sibs. Changes in relations with neighboring groups like the Gabrielino (Tongva), Luiseño, and Kumeyaay, and less frequently the Chemehuevi, Halchidhoma, Mojave, and Yuma, also affected social relations. In addition, epidemics of disease brought from Europe during the historic period decimated the Cahuilla population, eliminating entire sib groups and many lineages, and causing significant interruption of the precise social organization. Forcing children into government schools prevented the normal acculturation process necessary to maintain traditional economic practices. Government schooling provided a structural barrier which prevented children from journeying to favored gathering and food processing sites where they could learn the technical and social skills they would need to live in harmony with the environment and with each other. The practical reality of a people under outside pressure is the legacy of Columbus.

Despite the precise nature of historic Cahuilla social organization, the basic premise that the nature of all things is unstable has resulted in a tradition flexible enough to expand and contract to aid the survival of the current generation. After a period of population decline, Cahuilla population is again expanding. As it expands, there is a resurgence of interest in the old ways which had been partially or wholly abandoned. In the first half of this century, Cahuilla children turned to the game of baseball to satisfy the social function once fulfilled by the *peon* and other traditional games popular throughout southern California. Today, their grandchildren want to learn bird songs, the ancient songs that describe the migrations of the Cahuilla people and others.

Many Cahuilla people still practice some of the old ways of living. Some families still gather piñon together, an activity with social as well as economic elements. A woman, her sisters, aunts, and cousins and all of their children will go piñon harvesting together. Now, instead of using hot rocks to roast nuts in a pit oven, they use the radiation of a microwave oven.

Fast food, pharmaceutical medicines, baseball, cars, American English, and a host of other trappings of Western culture have been adopted by the Cahuilla, yet despite the pressure to adapt, there is still a clear Cahuilla identity. The thing which makes a person Cahuilla is not measured by clothing, food, housing, or a government enrollment number. The element which defines a person as Cahuilla resides in the heart. This volume is a revealing of that inner heart, a commentary by Cahuilla people on their culture and tradition.

THE UNIVERSITY OF CALIFORNIA, RIVERSIDE, the University of California Humanities Research Institute, the National Endowment for the Humanities, and the California Council for the Humanities all sponsored and funded the project from which this text in part resulted. Parts of it were originally conceived as a catalog for the traveling exhibition *Cahuilla Voices: We Are Still Here*. Invitations went out to the Cahuilla community, seeking people who would serve as a "focus group" to guide the project. The search brought five Cahuilla people and a cross-section of Cahuilla culture, in the persons of Katherine Saubel, Alvino Siva, Dolores Alvarez, Anthony Andreas, and JoMay Modesto. In addition, non-Cahuilla scholars were recruited to work on the project. During planning sessions for the exhibition, the focus group made decisions about what was important to say, and how it should be said. Sacred information was separated from the secular. History and tradition were examined. Modern attitudes and practices were compared with those of a century ago and those of pre-contact times.

The day-long discussions took place in July 1991, and were taped and subsequently edited. Unfortunately, when the State of California experienced its great budget crisis of the early 1990s, the budget for the catalog dissolved and until now, the catalog for the project was abandoned.

During the seven years this project has taken, I have been privileged to learn a tremendous amount about Cahuilla culture. But more important, I was witness to the acting out of the very essence of Cahuilla identity. Personal, political, and philosophical differences were put aside as the participants joined in the celebration and exposition of their common heritage. Differences sometimes ran deeply; but always, without exception, individual personalities were set aside and the group acted in concert, a reflection of an ancient coping mechanism, a successful strategy for continuing tradition. Today, as always, this is the road to survival as a people. It is the logical road to travel.

—*Deborah Dozier*

Participants

Katherine Saubel, an elder who lives at Morongo Reservation, has provided invaluable insight into the ancient traditions of ethnobotany and language, as well as family and social structure. She has testified in congressional hearings regarding

land use on reservations and has been a member of the state of California's Native American Heritage Commission since 1983. She is president of the Malki Museum, a museum of Cahuilla culture on Morongo Reservation. She is the author of several volumes including: *I'isniyatam* (An Interpretation of Cahuilla Designs); *Chem'ivillu'* (Let's Speak Cahuilla); and with Lowell J. Bean, *Temalpakh* (From the Earth), an ethnobotanical work for southern California. A list of honors and awards would fill several pages; she was appointed Regent's Lecturer at the University of California, Riverside, in Spring 1990; in 1994 she was inducted into the National Women's Hall of Fame, and was honored by the Smithsonian Institution, National Museum of the American Indian for her cultural contributions. She and Alvino Siva are sister and brother.

Alvino Siva was born and raised in Palm Springs. He calls his father's reservation, Los Coyotes, home although he lives in Banning. As a young man, he joined the military, leaving Cahuilla territory for twenty years. Upon his return he worked to resurrect bird singing, a culturally important art form; he now makes and sells beautiful rattles and teaches rattle making and bird singing to young and old, Cahuilla and non-Cahuilla people. He remembers the ancient culture heroes who formed the earth and fashioned culture, and tells their stories in both English and Cahuilla. He and his wife, Pat, ride horses along the old Cahuilla trails which connect the desert, the pass, and the mountains beyond. He and Katherine Saubel are siblings.

Dolores (Dee) Alvarez is an independent businesswoman from Cahuilla Reservation. She has been very active in Cahuilla tribal matters most of her adult life, working for many years to improve education and housing for Cahuilla people. She has served as Director of Education for the Soboba Band of Mission Indians, on Soboba Reservation in San Jacinto, California. She has also served as the Counselor Coordinator for the All Mission Indian Housing Authority. She holds an Eminence Credential in American Indian History and Culture. She and JoMay Modesto are sisters.

Anthony Andreas was born and raised in Palm Springs, where he is the past vice-chairman and tribal historian at Agua Caliente Reservation. He served as the tribal monitor for archeology for the Agua Caliente band for many years, and has monitored many archeologic surveys and digs in Tahquitz Canyon. He, too, is a bird singer and is dedicated to reconstructing the art form as it was in traditional times, from extensive notes left by his grandmother. He was actively involved in the creation of the Agua Caliente Cultural Museum, a center dedicated to Cahuilla culture located in Palm Springs.

JoMay Modesto, also an independent businesswoman, has served her community at Cahuilla Reservation in a variety of ways for many years. She is an enrolled member, has been involved in tribal administration for more than twenty years, and has served on the tribal council. She is a member of the Cahuilla Economic Advisory Council, a commissioner of the All Mission Indian Housing Authority, and the Cahuilla Reservation delegate to the Southern California Tribal Chairman's Association. She is currently the tribal monitor for a federal grant to develop tribal administration. She and Dolores Alvarez are sisters.

Dr. Lowell J. Bean, anthropologist and professor emeritus at CSU Hayward, and *Ken Hedges,* Chief Curator at the San Diego Museum of Man, were consultants to the project. Lowell Bean is fictive kin to many Cahuilla people, having worked and lived with them over the past thirty years. He has visited most of the museums and other institutions in the United States that have Cahuilla materials, and has acquired an intimate knowledge of Cahuilla material culture, social structure, faunal environment, ethnobotany, settlement patterns, ritual, law, and economic patterns. He has authored many volumes and papers, including *Mukat's People: The Cahuilla Indians of Southern California* and, with Katherine Saubel, *Temalpakh.* Ken Hedges is a southern California rock art specialist with extensive experience in field surveys and has been recording rock art sites in southern California from 1970 to date. He has prepared numerous specialized reports on topics including ethnobotany, land use and ownership practices and concepts, ethnohistory, rock art, and ethnoastronomy. He is the director of the annual Rock Art Conference. *Deborah Dozier* facilitated and recorded the conversations reproduced in the text.

Note

Throughout the text of this book, initials of speakers precede their comments. In alphabetical order by last name, they are:

DA	Dolores Alvarez
AA	Anthony Andreas
DD	Deborah Dozier
JM	JoMay Modesto
KS	Katherine Saubel
AS	Alvino Siva

PROLOGUE

This version of the Cahuilla creation story is a translation by Katherine Saubel of a recording made by a shaman, Perfecto Segundo, more than half a century ago. The text in italics has been added for clarity, since the story, which initially took an entire night to relate, has been greatly edited.

The story goes like this. There was night, only darkness. When they were going to appear, the night shook, the night vibrated. The night rang and then it quieted down. And then they appeared, just out of nothing. Just out in mid-air they hung. There was nothing to hold them up. They were just suspended in the air. Then they disappeared. That is when they say it was a miscarriage. And then it happened again. They appeared like they did, and they disappeared. And then they hung again, suspended in air. Then the thing they were suspended in dried. Then they moved. They moved and they stretched. They grew and they stretched some more.

In this way, the two gods, Mukat and Témayawet, were born from an embryo formed by primordial forces associated with darkness and the night, Tookmeoot and ʔamnaʔa. Mukat and Témayawet argue with each other about which of them was born first. Then they climb to the top of the centricle of the world. They draw the earth from their hearts, then the ocean and the sky. They connect the earth and the sky by fixing the centricle in the middle.

And then Témayawet asks again, "What are we going to do now?" And Mukat says, "You should know but you don't. So now we will create the people." Then they started to create the people. They did not get them out of their mouths, but they worked them from the mud. It was in the dark that they did all this. Témayawet created his creatures in a hurry and carelessly. Then he was finished. Mukat made his people slowly, everything was done slowly and everything was done perfectly. It was not like Témayawet had created his people, with webbed

> When they were going to appear, the night shook, the night vibrated.

19

And they shook, their hearts shook. They quivered from their power. Then they brought out the sun.

feet and webbed hands, with two faces—one in the back and one in the front. Mukat created them beautiful, just the way they are now with their hands, their feet, their eyes—everything beautiful, perfect.

And then Mukat said, "I wonder why Témayawet is finished. I wonder why he has done everything so quickly?" And then Témayawet told him, "How are we going to know? How are we going to see what we are doing? This is all in the dark. And so our hearts will bring out the stars and we will spray them up to the sky and then we will have light. And we will do this now." They started to shake. Their powers shook them. They vibrated, they thundered, and then the stars came out of their mouths. "Now we shall create the sun rays. Now we shall create the rays—the gray, the white rays of the sun." And they shook, their hearts shook. They quivered from their power. Then they brought out the sun.

When everything they had done was complete Mukat knew that Témayawet's creations were not too good. When the light shown on them, then Témayawet knew that he wasn't doing things the right way. The people were not formed the right way. Mukat told Témayawet, "You were older and yet you didn't do a very good job with your creatures, with your faces that look both ways, with their stomachs both ways, their hands all closed and webbed." It wasn't like the hands that Mukat made, with the fingers, the toes. "You said you were older," he said. "How are they going to carry? How are they going to carry their baskets? How are they going to carry their load, when they have a back on each side?" Mukat said, "When they gather or when they get and go and carry their game, they will have no place to carry it."

Then Témayawet said, "This way, when they go, they don't have to turn around, they don't have to do anything. Just do it both sides, both ways, and it will save them a lot of time."

But Mukat said, "Well, look at my creatures. They can close their fingers when they are going to carry water or hold something in their hands. They can turn around, they can look around, there is nothing in the way. They can carry anything on their shoulders."

Then Témayawet said, "Our creations won't die, they will live forever."

And Mukat said, "No, they will crowd the world.

That cannot be. We will have people to cure illnesses, but everyone must die."

When he sees how fine Mukat's creations are, Témayawet is ashamed of his own. He goes underground, taking his creatures with him, causing great earthquakes. But Ménill, the Moon, stays with Mukat.

Ménill stayed with him. Moon Maiden, he called her. The Moon Maiden took care of the creations. She took them and showed them games, how to make this from that, painted them and colored them. She put designs on them and made them dance. She just trained them in everything she could find. Then she would sing the songs to them. They would dance and they would kneel down and touch down. It was all of them together, not just one or two. She would make them do this.

But these beings were not ordinary people. They were beings that were supernatural. They had strength, they had power. And then there was the Moon Maiden. Then Mukat passed by Ménill, the Moon Maiden. The story says that Mukat overshadowed her. Moon Maiden had the feeling that something bad had happened. She could feel it. She felt bad. She never said a word to anyone, she didn't tell him she was going to leave them. But in the night, she left and went up to the sky. She never told anyone, she just left without telling them where she was going. The next morning, they looked for the one that she took care of. They looked for her. They cried. They went here and there and looked for her but they couldn't find her. There was a pool of water. They looked and saw her in the water, and they all jumped in there. But she disappeared. They saw her reflection from the sky. They looked up and saw her. They called her down. They told her, "When you were here we were happy. Everything was beautiful and wonderful and we miss you. Come on down." She just smiled at them.

Mukat becomes a menace rather than a help to his people. He has already put death into the world, and now he gives poison to the rattlesnake. He invents the bow and arrow and tricks people into shooting at one another. The souls of the dead wander, lost, to the four directions, until a super being comes and shows them the way to Telmikish, the land of the dead, and he shows the people the mourning rituals for the dead. The people become angry with Mukat.

The Moon Maiden took care of the creations. She took them and showed them games, how to make this from that, painted them and colored them. She put designs on them and made them dance.

They gathered together and they talked about how he was probably going to destroy us. They discussed this among themselves and decided they were going to get rid of him before something drastic happened to them. That was not just a few people, there was a lot of people at the time. They all agreed to do away with him.

The rituals for mourning the dead come from the Cahuilla creation myth. It concludes with an elaborate description of the death of the creator god, Mukat. No one now living is able to retell the myth in the traditional manner in the Cahuilla language.

At the beginning, the words are different. The ancient words that tell this story are different, it is deeper than what we are saying now. The ancient words were said before. "My children, my creatures, my created beings," he told each and every one, "I guess I am going to die," he said. He said, "My heart is getting cooler, my hands are getting colder." He was getting worse when he said this. Then he sang this song, "I guess I am going to die."

Mukat's long death scene takes up a major part of the myth. Much of Cahuilla ritual life connected to mourning and burial ceremonies is included in this part of the story. In his death song, Mukat enumerates all of his acts of creation and recites the names of all the plants and animals he has created. He teaches the people the sacred traditions that they are to live by.

"I feel it. I feel it. I am going to die." He was getting weaker and weaker. He said this to his creatures. Then he started to sing the song. He sang this and explained to them. He was saying this as he was singing this. His creatures sang with him. And they were singing for him as he was lying down and getting worse and worse.

Mukat is dead. This is where it ends. He is singing the song. "It is dropping on me, he is falling on me. It is getting old on me," he says, as he sings. "It is getting old on me, it is getting old on me. It is falling on me. It is singing, naming all the plants, falling on me. It is dying on me." This is where it ends.

The people burn Mukat's abandoned body. From Mukat's ashes, all the food plants grow—acorns, squash, chia, sage, all the food of the Cahuilla. In his death, Mukat has given his people their way of life, their laws, customs and ceremonies, and their food.

IDENTITY

DEBORAH DOZIER: How do you know you're Cahuilla?

KS: Because I speak the language. When you know your language, you know who you are.

DD: When was the first time you realized that you were Cahuilla, as different from an Anglo or a Frenchman, for example?

KS: Oh gosh. Oh, probably when I was about five years old, four years old. I know it was strange to me when I saw a white person for the first time. I thought they were just painted that white. I didn't know, really, that it was their regular skin. I guess it was because I was comparing that to my own. I said, "Oh, they must be painted white." [laughs]

I was born up in the mountains at Los Coyotes. Nobody came in there at that time, you never saw anybody. We moved to Palm Springs, and that's where I saw the first white man, in Palm Springs. My younger brother and my younger sisters, they were born in Palm Springs, and they grew up seeing the white people around there. It wasn't much of a shock to them because they knew they were there already. But it was to *me* when *I* first saw them [laughs].

AA: I know [I am Cahuilla] because I was told by my grandmother. I suppose she was told by her people. We were there all the time. We just grew up being Cahuilla. They call us Mission Indians, but she said, "We are *not* Mission Indians, we are Cahuilla." Besides being Cahuilla, we had another name. We were *Painiktum* clan. But we were Cahuilla as a whole. This was passed down.

AS: [Sighs] It is really hard when you are a little kid. When you really find out who you are is when you start to go to school, and the other children start making fun of you. They are calling you names, so then it is in your mind. When you get home, you ask your parents. I asked my dad, "Why are they

> It was strange to me when I saw a white person for the first time. I thought they were just painted that white. I didn't know, really, that it was their regular skin.
>
> —*Katherine Saubel*

23

Cabezon, c. 1890

This photograph is of Chief Cabezon, the son of the
famous nineteenth century Cahuilla leader for whom
Cabazon Reservation was named. The younger Chief
Cabezon was a political leader of the desert Cahuilla
between 1880 and 1900.

Collection of the Agua Caliente Tribal Museum

saying this to us, to me?" And my dad would say in Indian, "They don't know us Cahuillas." This is when they start telling you who you are. He said, "From the beginning, when they come here, they stole everything of ours; and now they refuse to know us. They don't really want to know us. That is why they are calling you those names." Then all of sudden you say, "Hey, I must be different," you know, other than just looking at yourself and you are colored different. Then you know. He would say, "The Cahuillas were great people, and the people that are making fun of you don't want to face it." This is when your pride starts coming in and when they start telling you these stories how great the Cahuillas are. Then you say, "Well, hey, I *am* all right." When you are little, you really don't know. You are just running around and playing with other kids. Then all of a sudden some of them turn against you and say you are a stinking Indian. Things like that, you know?

JM: When I read the tales of the Palm Springs Indians [*Stories and Legends of the Palm Springs Indians,* by Francisco Patencio] I went to ask my dad, "Is this why we did this and that?" It all jelled together as to what I really was. That is when I really, truly said, "I am Cahuilla, and I know." And I *was* all that time, but it was all scattered. Then it all jelled and made sense.

AA: To be Cahuilla... I never thought much about it being any different. I thought everybody had some ties with their past, whether they were Indian or not. And we just happened to be Cahuilla. If a Frenchman was a Frenchman, well that is what he was: a Frenchman. Everybody had their background and our background is Cahuilla. That is what I was told. They are told when they are growing up that they are French or whatever. How do you know you are French? How do you know you are English? Because you were told that. It was through oral histories passed down through the elders. They got it from their elders, and it passed on down. It is not something new that has been made up.

DD: Is it a complicated thing to be Cahuilla?

KS: Today I think it is. A long time ago it wasn't. It was

They don't really want to know us. That is why they are calling you those names.... The Cahuillas were great people, and the people that are making fun of you don't want to face it.

—*Alvino Siva,*
quoting his father

25

Identity

Victoria Las Weirick

This woman is demonstrating a hand and looped string figure, used to predict the gender of unborn babies. These cat's-cradle-like games were played for fun as well, the strings being manipulated by the fingers, hands, and wrists to form designs which represent metates, doorways, and other common forms.

Many people seem to want to be Indian. They think it is easy to be Indian. It's not, because there is a whole etiquette to it.

—JoMay Modesto

just a natural thing. It is just the way you were. But now, I think it is very hard.

JM: Many people seem to want to be Indian. They think it is easy to be Indian. It's not, because there is a whole etiquette to it. The individual as is so popular today doesn't exist for the Cahuilla in that sense. It's a community thing for the people.

DA: Sometimes they wake up in the morning and wish they were anything but Indian. You have to deal with this, you have to read about that, you know. There are so many things you have to know. Your state codes, your federal codes.

KS: Dee brought up something I don't think the public knows at all. She said it is really complex and hard to be an Indian because you have so many laws. It is like you are in two nations at the same time, with two totally different scripts you have to learn.

JM: It consumes your whole life.

AS: Everything had to be done right if you were going to do it. If not, then don't. After a while, we got away from that precision. Even cutting wood or picking up a rock, everything. You had to talk to it. But after a while, we got away from it. Now you can just go and do anything you want and you never even think about it, how you were brought up.

JM: I think what is *very* important is that we were always told if you were going to do something, you do it *right*. I think that was a big point of view of the Cahuillas, that if you were going to do something, you did the best you could do. It might not have been successful, but you gave it your best shot.

KS: And you don't have the language there anymore. You don't really know the way the Cahuillas were at one time. That is all disappearing. They asked me, "How many Cahuillas are there?" "Not very many," I said, "Maybe nine hundred, maybe close to that, maybe not even that." I am talking about the ones that are half, and the ones that are a quarter. That is the least that we can go to, the quarter. The rest of them are ones that are one-eighth, one-sixteenth, one-something. They are no more, nothing. That makes it hard. I think it all depends on your blood quantum, who you are. The more you have of Cahuilla blood, you are a Cahuilla.

DD: Are there any more Cahuillas who are really full blood?

KS: Oh, there is, here in this reservation, David Quatte, there is Joe Sabo, there is Eileen Johnson, and there is Josephine Johnson. Those are full-bloods. In our area, there is still quite a few ones that are still full. In Palm Springs, I don't think there is any full-bloods there anymore. The last one died—Flora Patencio, she was the last full-blood in Palm Springs. Out in the desert, there is more there. Like Robert Levi. Ooh, there is a whole lot of these Quattes and Morenos. They are all full-bloods.

DD: What do the rest of you think about being mixed and being Cahuilla? I know some Cahuilla say that if you don't have the language, if you don't have your father's lineage, if you weren't raised in and don't know all the traditions, then you aren't really Cahuilla.

AA: Well, I say if you weren't raised as a Cahuilla, if you were raised outside, you can be Indian through your roots. You have Cahuilla blood in you. You can't say, "You aren't because you wasn't raised." It is just a matter of opinion. Others say, "Well, you don't speak the language." My kids can't talk the language, but they know the bird songs, some of them. They grew up being Cahuilla. They know they're Cahuilla in their heart.

I was cleaning this lady's yard when I was twelve or fifteen years old, in town. She asked me if I was

> Everything had to be done right if you were going to do it. If not, then don't. After a while, we got away from that precision. Even cutting wood or picking up a rock, everything.
>
> —*Alvino Siva*

27

Fidel Norte, c. 1946

Fidel Norte herded cattle at Los Coyotes Reservation in
the 1940s. Cahuilla men worked on Spanish, Mexican,
and American cattle ranches as hands and as ranch fore-
men. Who would know better the locations of forage,
water, and deep shade? They used the skills learned from
contact with Anglo ranchers to start their own cattle
herds. Many Cahuilla still own cattle or lease their lands
for cattle grazing.

Collection of Alvino and Pat Siva

Indian, and I said "Yeah." She wanted to know what kind of food we ate. I said, "Beans, tortillas." She said, "That's Mexican food." I never thought of it as Mexican food, because I grew up with that. It bothered me. When I got older, it was easy—if a Mexican makes it, it's Mexican food. If an Indian makes it, it's Indian food. There is a little difference.

JM: You are what you are and you never really question it. You think everybody else is the same way. You know, if you are an independent thinker or a strong person, you assume that everybody else is, and you don't really think of yourself as being the exception. I think the Cahuillas were the exception. The fact that they had intuition, that they were, maybe, open to feelings, to their environment. They were unconsciously aware of what was going on in their surroundings, whether it be people or climate. You can feel—like you say, you can feel spring in the air. I think Cahuillas were really in tune with that, and not just with the climate but with the plants. They could sense that something might be wrong and they might look and think, "This blossom should be coming on this tree and it is not. What's wrong?" They were sensitive to other people's feelings. Like a weather vane; what is going on? Is there something in the air? Whether it be political change, dissatisfaction or contentment. I think they were really open to it. I go a lot on gut feeling. I think a lot of Cahuillas do. You know without being told.

DA: I always thought it was my talent [laughter]. And it wasn't, because I find that more and more Cahuillas can do that. You can pretty well assess everything the minute you walk into a meeting or you see somebody. You know when something is wrong. You know then how to respond. You pick and choose your words very carefully, because of how that person is going to interpret it. You have to be aware. As you are reading them, you are turning into your head to try to figure out how you are going to communicate, how you are going to react based on just how you feel about them.

JM: Have you read *Clan of the Cave Bear?* What interested me was her contention that this clan had

My kids can't talk the language, but they know the bird songs. They know they're Cahuilla in their heart.

—*Anthony Andreas*

29

Sylvester Saubel at about age 50, c. 1900

Sylvester Saubel was a powerful leader and the last Cahuilla eagle dancer. He was said to have "eagle eyes" and possessed an exceedingly piercing gaze.

Collection of the Smithsonian Institution

memories that were inherited through the genes, so that everybody was in tune to what they were because of their breeding. I thought that it sounded kind of dumb, but then I started thinking about it. I often wonder if that isn't the way it is with Cahuillas. That you know something without being told. You know instinctively what it is and you can pinpoint.

One of the feelings that I have, I can remember being at a funeral, at a *velorio* [wake], and I don't know the songs and I don't speak the language, but all of a sudden, during this one song, I had this real distinct feeling of just crying. Tears just welled up and they came out. There was a couple of other women that did the same thing. Later, in talking to some of the people, they said that was the "crying song." So it was the time when everybody was to feel that emotion. Why did I feel that emotion when I really didn't know what the song was?

In my memories of going home to Cahuilla Reservation... maybe Mom and Dad had a problem with something and we needed to go home from where we lived in Fallbrook. We would go and it was not unusual to find dinner cooked. They were expecting you. When you walked in they'd say, "What do you want? What is wrong?" They knew that you were coming, that there was a certain need.

My dad told me that my mom was having problems in Fallbrook. We went over to [Torres-] Martinez to get my godfather. They were having a funeral and he just was sitting there. He knew that he could not partake of the ceremony because he was waiting for my dad.

My dad walked in, and my godfather said, "When do we go?" He knew that he had to leave with my dad. I wonder if there isn't something within us... that intuition. We all kind of have that ability to think and to know what we need to do and to expect things. A lot of times you know what is going to happen before it happens. Or I know what that person is going to say before they say it. I don't think it is just me as the exception, it is a lot of Cahuillas. Some are more intuitive than others.

> You can pretty well assess everything the minute you walk into a meeting or you see somebody. You know when something is wrong. You know then how to respond. You pick and choose your words very carefully.
>
> —*Dolores Alvarez*

Identity

I wonder if there isn't something within us... that intuition. We all kind of have that ability to think and to know what we need to do and to expect things. A lot of times you know what is going to happen before it happens.

—*JoMay Modesto*

I felt that the other day. I was in the middle of cleaning my house and my cousin had just lost her son. It had been three weeks. I don't know—I put everything down and went to the phone and called my mom and asked her if she wanted to go visit Auntie. She said yeah, and we went down there to see my cousin. Sure enough, we went to her house and she was having a really bad time. There was a wedding and a lot of her family had gone there, all the kids. She felt it was too soon, and she felt really alone. It had been three weeks. I knew that my cousin needed me, needed that family support. I wasn't told, it was just the intuition.

AA: I think a lot of people have had experiences like that. I don't think I have personally, but I know when we used to go to ceremonies like that, women all of a sudden would start crying at a certain song, automatically. It was not only us. Other tribes, they have done the same things with their songs. I have even seen men cry, but I don't know if it was on account of the songs. These were ceremonial leaders, too.

Intuition! All I know is that my grandmother said that you have to do things a certain way. It just comes automatic after a while. I used to help my grandmother. She buried all her family on her side, and she buried my side. She was about the last one to go, and when she died I had to do that. I was lost. I did it anyway, it was automatic. When I started thinking about it, I didn't know what to do. But when I did, I thought I knew too much. It went to my head, because everybody said I did good.

We would go to different areas. We would go to Santa Rosa [Reservation], and we were all one people. And that one people is Cahuilla. We knew there were other tribes mixed in too, but basically it was all Cahuilla.

DD: And everything was done the Cahuilla way?

AA: Right. It wasn't explained to me that this is the Cahuilla way, we just automatically knew it.

Salvador Lopez, 1965

Salvador Lopez was famed for his ability to eat fire.
One woman recalls seeing him when she was a child.
"It was dark. He reached down into the bed of glowing
coals. He held up his hand, which was full of live coals,
and blew on them, filling the air with red sparks. Then
he put those coals in his mouth and blew. Smoke and a
shower of sparks flew from his mouth. He was never
burned."

Collection of the Malki Museum

"Cahuilla Indians at one of the Hot Springs," c. 1903

The Cupeños, a Cahuilla group that split off and began developing a distinct cultural several hundred years ago, lived at Cupa (Warner's Hot Springs) for many generations before the land was claimed by the Spanish, the Mexicans, or the Americans. Title to the land at Warner's was transferred to John Warner after the United States accessioned California in the mid 1800s. Cahuilla and Cupeño people continued to live there after the title transfer until 1903, when action was initiated to oust them from the land around the springs. Here a Cahuilla woman washes clothes at the spring, as her family had been doing for generations.

Photograph: Attributed to George Wharton James, who was famous for his early ethnographic work among the Cahuilla.

Collection of Southwest Museum, Los Angeles

FAMILY

KATHERINE SAUBEL: The Cahuilla family in ancient times was just wonderful. They had everything to gather. The women gathered the food—the seeds and the pods, whatever. The men hunted. They had a wonderful life.

It wasn't really dry here then, my father said. It was really green and luscious and they just lived in harmony. They had skirmishes when one went to another's area without asking permission. You had to ask permission—they weren't going to say no, but some of them just went in without asking and that's when they had skirmishes over their areas where they got food and things like that. So that's the only time. But otherwise they lived in perfect harmony and lived with their creator, the way he told them to live among each other and it was fine.

AS: I don't know if I told you about when they killed all the Sivas except that one boy. Down in Collins Valley… our village was there, we must have been a big clan there. Somebody, my dad wouldn't tell me who it was—the Diegueños* or somebody—they came at night and they killed all the Sivas while they were asleep, except one little boy. When they were running through the village killing everybody, an old lady, the grandmother, took this little boy and pulled his penis up between his testicles and hid it from these guys, these men that were doing all the killing, and she said, "Do not kill this one. This is a girl, when she comes of age you can have your fun." They spared that little boy. The grandmother took him and brought him to what they now call La Quinta.

She came over the mountain down there. The boy was raised down there in La Quinta. After the

> They had a wonderful life. It wasn't really dry here then, my father said. It was really green and luscious and they just lived in harmony.
>
> —*Katherine Saubel*

---

* The Diegueño, or Kumeyaay, are the native people of what is now the southern part of San Diego County.

Family

They would say we were
related to the bears....
They would say that when
you looked at him and he was
still dancing, all of a sudden
you would see a bear.

—*Alvino Siva*

Juan Siva with son and grandson, c. 1940

This photograph was taken outside the adobe home of
the Siva family in Palm Springs, near what is now the
Spa Hotel. Alvino's father built the home when the family moved from Los Coyotes Reservation in the mid-
1920s. The building was demolished years ago.

Adobe houses were common in the lowlands, where
rainfall was minimal. Brush housing was favored in the
mountains. Later, clapboard houses were common.
Today the Department of Housing and Urban Development is building frame houses on several Cahuilla
reservations.

Top to bottom: Alvino Siva, Juan C. Siva, Peter Siva
Collection of Alvino and Pat Siva

boy got maybe ten, eleven years old, those people would make fun of him because his people were killed. But it came out that he was a great shaman. He had a lot of power. When he came of age, he probably killed a lot of people by using his power.

He was the one that could turn himself into a bear, this guy. So after he became a man, he moved his people from there to Elgowaltah. They said that was where he grew up and became a man and raised his family. I guess the clan got bigger. Then they would go into Collins Valley, back to our old place there. That was where they stayed in the wintertime. They would move up there.

They would say we were related to the bears. That is where the greatness came on our part, but this was a long time ago. The younger ones don't know about this.

My dad said if it wasn't for that ancestor I wouldn't be here now. I don't know how many hundreds of years ago this happened. This is a long time ago.

He said this guy was really powerful. Right there in Collins Valley, I guess they were having a drought there, and people were dying of starvation. I guess the rain people couldn't bring the rain to grow anything. One day the geese were flying over. But he said this guy, my great-great-grandfather, surrounded them with heat by using his power and brought the geese down. Everybody had a feast.

They said they used to see when he would carry the first son of his. They say they would see a bear going up the canyon somewhere with the little boy sitting on the thing. That was his father, the bear. That is why we are related to the bear, so close. We can't even eat bear meat because you are eating your own kin. He said when they used to dance he would make noises like a bear. They would say that when you looked at him and he was still dancing, all of a sudden you would see a bear. When he would completely change, you would see a bear dancing. They said he would disappear and then turn back into himself. Like I tell the white people, it is hard to believe. It is hard to believe. The only way you can believe that is if you are an Indian, because not only

Like I tell the white people, it is hard to believe. . . . The only way you can believe that is if you are an Indian.

—Alvino Siva

37

Family

Each village had its own moiety, either the Coyote or the Wildcat. So the man had to go to a village of the opposite moiety to bring back his wife, and that's the way it was.

—*Katherine Saubel*

the Cahuilla, but other Indians I have talked to, like the Northwest Indians, they had people that would do that too, they had the power. We believe it because we know. When our elders tell us this is what happened, we believe them.

DD: How was the family structured?

KS: Well, the family was structured, in that they had their village. Each village had their leader, which was called the *net*. He had his messenger or his lieutenant, you might say, called the *paha*. He was the one who went from place to place and carried the message to the people: what they were supposed to do; how they were supposed to act; and if there was something that had to be done, he was the one who gathered all the people to talk to them.

And in that village, in each house the father was responsible for the family. Mother and father, any children they had. Sometimes the grandmother and grandfather lived with them, if they had no place else to live. Otherwise they had their own house. And they were protected, they were given food even when they were old. That's one of the things that I have often admired about my people, because in that way they never had an orphan. Nobody was neglected, because the family was so close. They were related so close. Like if there were two brothers and one had children and the brother with children died, the other brother became responsible for those children. Because they were his children, too. And he fed them and he took care of them. So they were always taken care of. They always would help one another.

DD: So all the people in the village would be your very close relatives? And would you be related to people in other villages too?

KS: Oh yes. Especially by marriage, because no one could marry a person from the same village, they were related too close. From one village the man had to go to another village, which was opposite to his moiety. He would go to that other, opposite village. Each village had its own moiety, either the Coyote or the Wildcat. So the man had to go to a village of the opposite moiety to bring back his wife, and that's the way it was.

JM: I think the focus was on balance—how everything had to be maintained in balance. Everything had its place. A time for everything. I think Cahuillas, having the need for survival in a harsh and unpredictable place, had to have that balance and control. Everything was centered around that which gave unity and balance and stabilization to how everything was run.

That impresses me—the ability to think and negotiate and to try to maintain a balance as opposed to an upheaval. I think that was the whole thing, that nothing should be out of balance. If there was a problem within a family or within a tribe, it was to be balanced out. The social problems were to be solved and everything was to be maintained. I think it even goes back to the control of who you married and how you married. It sounds kind of almost like what Hitler planned—a perfect society by having perfect people. So much emphasis was put on who you married. Not because of the prestige and social part of it, but because of the breeding. The children produced from that union would have good genes to be able to carry all of those needed attributes, whether it be thinking skills, physical skills, everything.

Basically, everybody that was a part of the community had to be contributing. You were groomed to whatever part of society you were needed in— maybe a leadership role, a medicine woman, a basket maker. If you were a good hunter you were groomed to be that, and you added to the society.

DD: When did traditional family structure change and what took its place?

KS: I always talk about the Cahuilla culture that's passed, that is no longer being carried out. It was very important. We have some remnants left of it that we still take care of. It's our religion, really, that we live by. That's the thing that we follow. The laws that were given to us by our Creator and the laws that were given to us by the Moon Maiden. All those had to be observed and [the laws] really guided them in the beginning and when the old people were still here. The ancient people followed that closely.

> Basically, everybody that was a part of the community had to be contributing, and you were groomed to whatever part of society you were needed in.
>
> —JoMay Modesto

39

Sherman Indian School, c. 1911

Indian students line up at Sherman Indian school in military-style uniforms. A military school model was used at Sherman; the main thrust was to separate the students from their cultures. As in White schools of the era, corporal punishment was used to discipline students. Indian students were punished for speaking Indian languages and running away from the schools, a frequent occurrence among children who were needed at home and preferred to be there.

The replacement of native language with English was a terrible blow to Indian culture. Today the Cahuilla are struggling to retain and revive their language as the number of native speakers declines with each generation.

The word "dead" written across the chest of one little girl and numbers on the chests of the others reflect an attempt at a later time to identify the children in the photo. A pediatric neurologist who examined the photo said the girl who died showed evidence of a genetically transmitted disease similar to muscular dystrophy.

Collection of the Sherman Indian School Museum

Now, when the non-Indians came into our land and took some of our rituals away… they just cut it out inch by inch, you might say, and now there is just a little bit left. And that's what happened. So every time somebody came here and changed our ways there was always something taken away from us and little by little we have lost it. There is just a remnant that we are hanging onto right now.

But it is still very important to us elders—to me, because I was raised traditionally and I know what is being lost. That's what really bothers me. The younger Cahuillas no longer live by the laws that were given to us, which we should have carried out if we weren't interrupted by the non-Indians.

I think that family structure probably changed drastically in about the 1880s and especially the 1890s, and clear into the 1900s. At the time, the government had more influence—the influence came closer to us here at the time. A lot of children, when they were young, were taken away to schools.

The idea of the government was to assimilate us to the white society. They wanted to turn us into white people. That can't be done because a lot of them were raised like I was, and they already had their own way, their life. It is very hard to assimilate to something else. But that was the whole purpose—to get the children, send them to schools, tell them not to learn their language, to forget their language and their culture and then go into present society. But it didn't work out that way, that's why we are still here. That's why a lot of us still speak our language.

So that's the way it was. But the whole idea of the federal government was to destroy us. Anyway, he found out what to do, to take all the land that we had and we had nothing. Later on, after they set aside the reservations, they made them into allotments.* They did that because while the Indians could not sell tribal lands, they could sell their allotments if they wanted to. And if they would all

> Every time somebody came here and changed our ways there was always something taken away from us and little by little we have lost it.
>
> —*Katherine Saubel*

---

* During the era of its "Termination" policy, the U.S. goverment terminated its trust responsibility to many reservations, alloting parcels to the families who lived on the reservations.

Sherman Indian School Banjo, Guitar and Mandolin Club

This 1917 photo exemplifies government efforts to assimilate Indian students into the dominant, white culture.

Collection of the Sherman Indian School Museum

sell them, there would be no more reservation. The Indian people would have to cope by themselves. That was the whole idea—never to help them but to really destroy them. That was the idea of the government. And he is still at it right now.

DA: I know the stories I heard—where some children were fighting over wood rats—my dad said that was when all the Cahuillas got mad. The parents got mad, and we have had factions ever since. I think that kind of started breaking things down. It was a lot easier to go to work and buy a loaf of bread than it was to worry about making sure that you got along with your neighbors so you could go out there and gather and get things together. The whole thing just broke us up.

Now, we have to go out, we want everything that everybody else has. We want to have those Pampers, and all that stuff. We go to work and we are not dependent any more. No more is there that tribal communal feeling.

AA: The Indian's traditional life was breaking up. They probably didn't know it then. Looking back, that's what happened. When my grandmother was growing up, that was Indian life as she knew it. It was quite different before she was born, I'm sure. The same with my dad. Each generation changes. Somehow, something is going along with the Indian way.

JM: Like any other family, it changes. It changes with TV and Nintendo games and whatever. It is not any different than the regular American family that used to sit around the table at night. Now, it is TV trays probably, in front of the TV instead of all having dinner together.

AA: There is a hard way and an easy way. If the Indians knew the easy way, they would do it. It is like basket and pottery making. That was all they knew. Once they got an easy way to replace what that was used for, they gave it up. Rifles came into existence. Everybody wanted a rifle instead of a bow and arrow.

It was like everybody else. I don't think it is much different. Maybe sometimes, but I think there are others, non-Indians, who think the same way. We are all human beings, after all.

Well, in the Cahuilla family, we were very close. Now it seems like we are being separated, because we have different lifestyles. When I was growing up, we were in close touch with my grandmother's people in Coachella. My great-grandfather had an adobe house right there outside of Coachella. My grandmother's sisters used to come over or we would go to visit them. One lived in Cabazon reservation, and the other one lived in [Torres-] Martinez someplace. We were related to the Levis. My grandmother was a Levi. And her mother was a Tortes from Santa Rosa [Reservation]. We kept in touch. She would come to visit the Torteses in Banning—Rafael Tortes—all the time. We had this family relationship. And all the ceremonies we used to go to in Morongo [Reservation], wherever, all different families and relations would be there. At funerals, all different types. Grandmother used to have ceremonies where they would just feed the Big House [ceremonial house]... and people would come. But we had this closeness that I don't think anybody else had, because we never left this area.

> If the Indians knew the easy way, they would do it....
> Rifles came into existence. Everybody wanted a rifle instead of a bow and arrow.
>
> —*Anthony Andreas*

Pedro and Maria Chino, c. 1900

Maria Chino is probably making a basket for sale. Basketry was a traditional skill useful in the white world. Cash earned by selling baskets to collectors gave Cahuilla women some economic independence. Metal buckets had largely replaced baskets and ceramic ollas as utility items in the Chino home by the time of this photograph.

Collection of the Palm Springs Historical Society

DA: Families were very, very important, and children were the ultimate. Your spouse comes first all the time in other cultures. In the Indian culture, when I was married to an Indian man, his children came first, after that his parents came first, and then you came. I liked that. That's the way it should be, and I respected him for that. He made those choices—to really take care of his mom, because she was older, and of course the children because they were younger.

A woman should be strong enough and able to take care of herself. An Indian woman doesn't go all the time to ask her husband everything that has to be done, or so I understand, at least where I came from. I can't speak for all Indian people. Most Indian women are so independent— even though they are not aggressive, and they are not saying a heck of a lot, they are still very opinionated and have their way of doing things. They feel good in making decisions. They make the decisions and the husband usually respects that, instead of coming in and saying, "Well, you should have done it this way," or making her feel like she was floundering out there. He supports her. The family was an important part of the whole system.

I think one difference is that we were more extended. Now that I have my children and my grandchildren and I am enjoying my nieces and my great-nieces and my great-nephews, I put them all on an equal basis. I love my great-nieces as much as I love my granddaughter, and there is no difference. Your grandmother, your aunt, they were all mothers. Everybody contributed a special portion that a child needed. Like my daughter has a special relationship with my mother, a special relationship with her aunt, a special relationship with her cousin. Her cousin is like a sister, her aunt is like a mother, her grandmother is like a combination of all three. Everybody contributes whatever my daughter needs at that time. She will go to one with a problem as opposed to just coming to me. I feel no jealousy for that.

JM: My kids have gone to Dee [Dolores Alvarez] and talked with her—more sometimes than with me. I

Families were very, very important, and children were the ultimate.

—*Dolores Alvarez*

45

Threshing beans, c. 1900

In the late 1800s large-scale farming was adopted by the Cahuilla. Here a family in Cahuilla Valley is photographed threshing beans. Notice the handmade wooden rakes and the use of burden baskets, burlap sacks, and a metal tub to hold the harvest.

Collection of the Smithsonian Institution

think it is really neat, because it just doesn't fall on one person. Everybody, like I say, has a different contributing part of it. That is what is neat.

We recently had a real tragedy in our own family. My cousin's son was in a fatal car accident. He was pronounced brain dead at the accident. He was taken to the hospital in San Diego and put on a life-support system—basically, for the sister to come from Hawaii and also so he could become a donor. The parents allowed for him to have most of his organs donated. I walked into the hospital and the whole lobby was full of cousins and aunts, and there was no distinction. Everybody stayed with him for days. Everybody took their turns and he was never left alone. Somebody was always holding his hand, and with him, and supporting all of the family. Even the nurses wrote a really neat letter. I was talking to one of them and she said, "I gave up trying to figure out who the mother was, the grandmother, the sister, the friend." [laughs] Everybody just gathered and contributed what they could to it. Everybody was on an equal basis, and I don't see a lot of that in other families. It was a hard time.

It was really an experience to actually see it in motion, actually being played. I think that was the way it would have been traditionally. Even now when you have a death everybody comes. Everybody knows what they have to do and everybody knows what they are good at doing. One family is there supporting, and cooking for that family so they don't have to worry about whether the kids are fed. Somebody from another family will be coming in and bringing dishes, or cooking, and taking care of those little extra things so the family can concentrate on what they have to do. That is lacking in the modern non-Indian world. Death or tragedy is never something that you experience by yourself. Everybody comes together in support. It is almost like when you hear of elephants having a death or a birth and they all gather in a circle, in a union of protection. I think that is what Cahuillas do.

When there was a birth there was an opening of the family to include a new child—to respect what that child can contribute. Or when there was a marriage, you didn't act like a typical mother-in-law or sister-in-law, whatever. You tried to invite them into the family—which was hard a lot of times. My mom, who was a Luiseño,* was never really approved of by my aunts. She wasn't liked, but yet because of the children, they had to put up with her. So a lot of times, they didn't say things. A lot of times they did, but you couldn't break that unit. The unit came before your own personal feelings.

DA: I think the whole thing is respect, because you care so much about those nieces and nephews that are out there. They are part of that unit. There was no jealousy. There was no reveling in the fact that a sister might be having problems. As a unit they try to figure out, "How we are going to work this out as a family?" Indian families are real protective and not willing to put down a relative. They will come to their defense.

> Most Indian women are so independent—even though they are not aggressive, and they are not saying a heck of a lot, they are still very opinionated and have their way of doing things.
>
> —*Dolores Alvarez*

47

Cahuilla woman grinding corn, 1923

Acorns were pounded in a mortar using a pestle.
Corn was ground on a metate using a mano like the
one pictured here. Notice the work basket perched on
the brush wall.

Photograph: Attributed to George Wharton James
Collection of Southwest Museum, Los Angeles

JM: The aunts are more protective than the mothers. You don't mess with them or they will get physical [laughter]. They will put you in your place real quick, and if you don't take that they will physically confront you.

DA: And then respect for a sister's boyfriend or a cousin's husband, you respect that person and always remember that they are part of that unit. So you don't have a lot of jealousies within the adults—female/male kind of jealousies that you can see happening sometimes.

JM: Sometimes the introduction into the unit is limited. You are allowed to come into the circle, but on a limited basis. You are not in the full middle circle or the actual center circle. You are given the opportunity to eventually be there. It is in very subtle ways, sometimes more direct. Sometimes it is depending on the character of that person who comes in. Of course, if it is another Cahuilla, then you normally understand that. Like Dee was saying about her husband—his family, his children, come first, and she came third. She knew that's the way it was and she had no problems with it.

DD: How are Cahuilla children raised?

JM: Around five years old is when you start exploring and they let you go ahead and do something. You are now old enough to start contributing something. But before that time, you are a precious commodity and you feel it. You feel so precious, and just something so special. You can just bounce around and go to a tribal meeting where everybody is at and feel like a treasure.

DA: Everybody knows who you are and they will give you candy or money, a hug, or a special place.... They remember something about you. They remember your name. I had a cousin that would be considered like an aunt, she was a cousin to my father, she knew everybody's name. She knows when most of their birthdays are, when they are coming into an age—school age or if they are going to be graduating from high school. She keeps track of them.

Your grandmother, your aunt, they were all mothers. Everybody contributed a special portion that a child needed.

—*Dolores Alvarez*

---

* The Luiseño homelands are southwest of the Cahuilla area, mostly in what is now northern San Diego County.

Family

Everybody knows who you are and they will give you candy or money, a hug, or a special place.... They remember something about you.

—Dolores Alvarez

Sometimes it was difficult for me because you have those boys that are "Boy" in the family. That is their name—Boy—and they have that special honor. They can be in the family and not contribute, but boy, when they come in it is like here comes the king. You guys get up and he is the male and he has everything all right there. It was hard for me as a young girl, not only to give up that position—because there I was being spoiled and my throne was taken away—but also, I guess, because I was a woman. That was part of it, too—because he was a male he came in and automatically got to sit at the head of the table. I would have a little side stool next to my grandmother [laughter]. And that is part of growing up. That is what you realize—you had your time and you have to give it up sometimes. It is interesting.

AS: My father, he didn't stand for any excuses and he was really strict. He wouldn't spare the rod. I think back now and I see I deserved it. But then he was really a nice, easy-going guy.

When I was growing up, my mother was the one that used to say to me, when I wanted to be lovey-dovey, you know how kids would grab their mother? I guess it was different with the Cahuilla or any other Indian people, because she would say, "No, you are a boy, you don't do that. Eventually you are going to be a man." My father would come sometimes and want to hug me and I would push him away and say, "No, I don't want that." He would laugh. But my mother said that mothers didn't do that to the boys because you are a man. Only the girls were held and loved. This is the side that a person would never believe that my father would come and do—come and hug you—because he was a really strict guy.

JM: Everything was kept in balance. Not just yourself so that you were safe and secure, but it was the family that was stable, and the tribe itself. Within your environment you didn't just take. What goes around comes around. There is an old saying in Cahuilla, a song that probably said the same thing in a different way. What you give will come back to you. If you give good it will come back to you. If

50

you give bad it will come back to you. So you always have to give in every part of your life, whether it be to a relationship, whatever. You extend yourself and it will come back to you at the time you need to have that support.

DD: So then you always need to be questioning your motives?

DA: Yeah, why do you do this, what is your reason?

JM: If you stop and think about it, are you doing it for jealousy or for your agenda? You know, your own gratification? Yeah. You better stop and think about it really good. Otherwise, it might not be good and something will come back to you.

DD: One of the main messages I hear is that you can trust your family. No matter what, you can trust your family.

JM: They were there. That is one of the neat things that probably makes me who I am—I don't really have to worry about not having a place. I really feel for people that are homeless—they not only don't have a home, they have no family to take them in. A lot of times in Indian families, it wasn't just the cousins and whatever, there was always somebody else that would be there. A cousin of a cousin or somebody else. And not just someone down on their luck. They just went there and stayed—maybe just an aunt that was older and maybe was widowed...

DA: That was everywhere. You could go to Banning, to Morongo, down towards [Torres-] Martinez. Right now I could go to Rincon [Reservation], I can go to Pala [Reservation] and you know people. You can stay a week, you can stay two weeks—and Indian people did that.

DD: And during those two weeks you would be a contributing member of that family unit?

JM: Yes, for as long as you are there. You assume a role.

DA: You had a place.

JM: It was not just here, you can go throughout southern California and find family. We were lucky, because my mom coming, from San Diego County, extended the family even more. She was Luiseño from Rincon.

We would go down to Palm Springs and stay there. When I married Marvin from Santa Rosa

> What you give will come back to you. If you give good it will come back to you. If you give bad it will come back to you. So you always have to give in every part of your life...
>
> —JoMay Modesto

Family

[Reservation] and we decided to move home to Santa Rosa, he asked me if I would have a problem there. My dad was raised with them. My godfather lived there and he was baptized in the church. It was like home. I had no problem with that. It was really neat. His family would extend to other people down towards Martinez. I would have a family gathering and there would be people there I had never met before. You never questioned it. They were welcome because they were with the other family. Sometimes they might even be non-Indian. They would be just as welcome and accepted.

THE LAND

ALVINO SIVA: They used to say *demron,* which means "This is your land. Don't make fun of it. Respect it."

AA: Originally each lineage had their own territory, their own land. We had our own territory. That's where my grandfather grew up—in a village called Rincon. It was right below Andreas Canyon.* It was a farming community. His father had started it, Juan Andreas. He was the captain. That was from about 1850 to 1895. When Captain Juan Andreas died my grandfather was about twenty years old. He moved to Morongo. His mother moved to Torres [Martinez]. She married a Levi, but they didn't have any kids. A lot of Andreases are buried in Torres, and some in Morongo.

DD: How long has your family been in Andreas Canyon?

AA: Since the beginning of time. They are the original lineage from that canyon and that surrounding area. It goes all the way up to the top of the mountain, the San Jacinto mountain.

DD: Before the Cahuilla were there, who was there?

AA: Well, I don't know. I heard this story from Joe Patencio, who told me that when the people left the Palm Springs area, according to the bird songs— which is what they are all about—they went into Mexico and back again. They came back and there was other people living here. They knew that this was our original territory, but they wouldn't leave. There was a battle, and they were chased out. I don't know if that is with the bird songs, or if it is a separate story. I don't think it is in the bird songs, but there was people here. [I've heard] that a lot of the rock art was there before we got there. But it could have been rock art that the original Cahuillas had made and came back and had forgotten about. No one knows. A lot of speculation.

> I felt real close to the canyons because that was where my people lived. . . . I could feel others there, but not seen. I wasn't scared of it. I felt I was a descendant and they weren't going to hurt me.
>
> —*Anthony Andreas*

---

* This Rincon village below Andreas Canyon is not to be confused with Rincon Reservation in northern San Diego County

Palm Canyon, 1924

Palm Canyon stretches southward through the Santa
Rosa Mountains all the way to Vandeventer Flat. The
trail through the canyon was an important link in a complex of trails over which people moved in, out of, and
through Cahuilla territory. Trails led to Santa Rosa village, to Piñon Flat, a major piñon harvesting area, and
westward to the coast. Hot and cold freshwater springs
dotted the canyon, as did palms. Because of its rare natural beauty, there have been many proposals to develop
Palm Canyon as a national park or for private use.
Strong tribal opposition to these suggestions has helped
keep the canyon available for future generations to enjoy.

Photograph: Edward S. Curtis
Collection of Southwest Museum, Los Angeles

I felt real close to the canyons because that was where my people lived. That's where we used to go in the evenings sometimes. There would be nobody there. I felt this closeness. I could feel others there, but not seen. I wasn't scared of it. I felt I was a descendant and they weren't going to hurt me. I feel that at the ranch too. I feel... It doesn't make me uncomfortable, it doesn't make me scared. I just know that they are there. They are not to bother me, this is their home before I was born. A lot of people would get scared. A lot of people have seen things at the ranch, seen people walking and there was nobody there. I have even heard my name called during the day and there was nobody around. I was sober. At night, sometimes I stay there by myself and I can hear my grandmother in the kitchen. Or she will call me and I would wake up. Oh, it's only Grandma. She just wants me to know that she is still here.

DD: What is the mouth of the canyon like? I have never seen it.

AA: Well, there are a lot trees. Running water, you can hear it. It is real peaceful. There are cottonwoods, sycamores, palm trees, and there is a ceremonial area that the shamans used at one time. There is a bedrock mortar, and cremation/burial grounds close by. My grandmother said it was Andreas [family] before they started burying. There is a burial ground at the flats. That was Rincon, my great-grandfather's village. I think that was where he was buried.

KS: The land's the most important thing. If you don't have land, you have nothing. And this land, to us, the Indian people, just doesn't mean a piece of land. This is a sacred area. This was given to us by our creator, to take care of it, to live here in harmony with it, and that's why we were put here—to protect it. But it's not happening because it doesn't belong to us anymore. They took it away from us and now it is going to be destroyed by all kinds of pollution. We are probably now in our last stages. Not only just the Indian people, but everybody else. Destruction is going on against the mother earth. Everything is being destroyed. Everything is being poisoned, your water, your lakes, and everything

> The land's the most important thing. If you don't have land, you have nothing.... This was given to us by our Creator, to take care of it, to live here in harmony with it, and that's why we were put here—to protect it.
>
> —*Katherine Saubel*

Old man Pedro Chino used to say, "This land is alive. It is alive." In Cahuilla, what he was saying to me is that the heart is fire, the heart of the land. He said, "That is why you can see where it breathes."

—*Alvino Siva*

else. Even the ocean is being spoiled now. All these things. The ocean is sacred water to us. But it is being polluted with everything you can think of.

AS: The old people said, "Before you, there was people that had this land and they took good care of it. That means it was passing on to you and you are going to have to treat it the same way." I remember that when my dad gave me that land down below, that's where they (his father I think) used to garden. This is where he used to do his gardening. But I haven't done any gardening. I have just used it for a pasture.

The land is close to the people because, as old man Pedro Chino used to say, "This land is alive. It is alive." In Cahuilla, what he was saying to me is that the heart is fire, the heart of the land. He said, "That is why you can see where it breathes." Like in Montana where that steam comes out. "If it doesn't," he said, "it will blow up." It had to breathe, the earth.

Pedro Chino would go down underground into the springs. He said, "To me it is just like this [he indicates the air] down in the ground."

But that was because he was the shaman of all shamans and he knew what he was talking about.

He told me about that water baby. That is what they called it. He said it lives down there. He said that is why it is at home down there. I don't know what happened to that water baby that used to wander there. Now they got a house building over the top of his spring. I don't know if he ever comes out or if he moved. He must be happy because if he wasn't, he would move that water, that spring.

Yeah, we have another there at our place, where that little water baby lives. You can hear him cry at night. It sounds like a little baby crying. Nobody sees it. If you see it or you say you see and you hear it crying, something is going to happen to your family somewhere, your relatives.

Like you were saying the other day, Pedro Chino was saying there is a reason for everything. It is the same way with everything, he said. And too, when you live in your house a long time, he says, it comes alive, like you. It is part of you, in other words,

Pedro Chino, 1938

Pedro Chino was a Cahuilla *pa'vu'ul*, the most powerful
of shamans. Pedro Chino was said to be able to travel
beneath the earth through the vents and channels con-
necting the many hot springs in the area. So skillful was
he, that he could travel from Palm Springs beneath
Taquish hehki (Mount San Jacinto) to the springs in
Soboba on the far side of the mountain peaks.

Collection of the Agua Caliente Tribal Museum

> We came from the land, from the earth itself. And it was created especially for you and so you had a place within that, and you were going to go back to it. There was always an attachment to it.
>
> —*JoMay Modesto*

your house. That is why he said we feed our house. That is the Big House, our ceremonial house, I am talking about. It is alive. Same way with your house. I remember it when I was growing up when I was living with my mother. We would be in the kitchen and she would feel a drop of moisture on her arms. You could see it. She would say, "My house is crying." That is what my mother used to say.

DD: Did the Cahuilla own the land communally?

KS: Yes, it was like I said. They created the land for us here, and gave it to us here. The North American continent was where all the Indians were at one time. Indians are now being killed off in some other areas, like South America. But as far as we are concerned, we are hanging onto ours here. Because it is so much, the land that is sacred to us. We are supposed to protect it. We are supposed to take care of it and live here and use the things that were put here for us. When we take care of it, it will take care of us. If we don't, we will be gone.

JM: The land was important. Mainly because it gave everything that you needed to live on. Well, we came from the land, from the earth itself. And it was created especially for you and so you had a place within that, and you were going to go back to it. There was always an attachment to it. And so it was important to be able to know your boundary. And we had definite boundaries. We know that, that was ours. You could look and see it and feel it. It was your responsibility. You became very protective of it. Even now.

I guess maybe it goes back to just my way of being brought up, that there are changes. The land will change, but it will always remain, it will always be there. It will take care of you. I guess that's what Daddy emphasized with us—to let this land take care of you. You can use it, but you try not to abuse it. You are going to change it, while it is taking care of you. You are going to change it, but it will remain.

DA: You know, when we started the sand and gravel [business] and we were digging all the holes up and everything, it was really devastating. It wasn't an easy decision. Even today, I don't like to look at the parts that are scarred and opened up. I remember one day being home and looking at the land and thinking, "It is a good feeling to look at it and see it and be able to sit on that rock and be able to realize that maybe five generations sat on the same rock and saw the same thing that I am looking at now. It is unchanged." But five generations are nothing compared to where you actually came from. It changed even from my dad. It changed even more so from when my grandfather was confined to a certain area.

You kind of look at the land and you talk to it. I did. I told the land that it is going to change. I have changed, my children are going to change. It doesn't mean that I disrespect you for who you are or what you have contributed to my life, but you are going to change your appearance. But I will always respect you for being there.

DD: And it is still giving you a living?

JM: Yes. I hope it will accept that. I guess that's the way they used to go out, and I don't know if the Cahuillas did it or not, but the Indians when they'd go hunting the coyotes, they prayed and they talked to it before they killed it and took it, realizing, "I am going to use that resource, I have to use that resource to continue." And it is what Cahuillas are. A lot of Cahuillas or other people don't realize that there is change, there is progress. Nothing stays the same. It is always changing, ever changing. You have got to be able to go with that. If you can't adapt to it, then you will go bananas.

DA: Land gives you power, more than just the power of ownership. I can look at Thomas Mountain, Santa Rosa Mountain, Cahuilla Mountain. We don't own that anymore, it is not within our jurisdiction, but it is still very much a part of me. When we were at the Big House in Cahuilla Reservation, when we would stay with our aunts, no matter where we were we could look up and see Cahuilla Mountain. It is still a focus of my life. I get strength from it when I see it. Just knowing that it is there, that it always has been and always will be. It is changing, just the natural erosion of it. But also it gives you a power, a personal power to the land. The land is your strength and you take care of it.

> People don't realize that there is change, there is progress. Nothing stays the same. It is always changing, ever changing. You have got to be able to go with that.
>
> —JoMay Modesto

59

I can sit on a rock and think ... how many hundreds of generations of Cahuillas have sat on that rock and thought, "This is mine, this is where I come from."

—*JoMay Modesto*

Yeah, you are going to change it, but you are also making it productive. We are starting to feel good about where we are at. We have had the sand and gravel excavated. But now we are smoothing it out and we are replanting it. So you see, it changes with us, it is becoming productive. I think that is the whole key to Cahuillas, is that if it is productive you do it. That productiveness means survival, and that you are going to continue to be in existence as people.

JM: You get a lot of personal strength from it. Not just the material power and the economic power to be able to control your own destiny. It goes right to you, to that ground. To what you can remember. It gives you that strength. You think, "I am part of this immense, mysterious, grand thing." You become a part of it. It gives you a lot of personal strength to your character. It is moving. You can go out and heal yourself with it. You go out and give thanks to it.

Actually, like a plant, you grow from it. You produce, you die, and you go back into it and another comes, which will be another generation. Hopefully, that feeling will stay. I see our children as being very protective and attached to it. Our responsibility is to make it so that there will be a place for them to come to. Luckily, from the very beginning of time, we have had a place that the Cahuillas have been able to look to.

I can sit on a rock and think how many generations, how many hundreds of generations of Cahuillas have sat on that rock and thought, "This is mine, this is where I come from." Not "mine" in the sense of possessing it, but "mine" in that I am a part of it, my world. And to be able to know that it is going to be there. To maintain it so that five generations, ten generations down the road, somebody will sit at that same rock and have the same feelings.

AA: Well, I think the Cahuillas and other Indians were the first conservationists.

DD: How do you mean?

AA: They didn't grow the plants, but they tended to them. Pruned them, trimmed them. They used to clean out underneath the trees. They cut out the underbrush to make it more fertile. They weeded. Even the mesquite tree, they pruned it. They took care of it. They just didn't wait until it blossomed.

KS: Yes, a long time ago when they took care of the areas where things grew, I remember the old people in Palm Springs saying that when they depended on it for a lot of the food, if it got any kind of bugs or insects that would destroy it, they would burn that. But they watched it, they didn't let it burn down. They just burned it enough to kill off these things. And they took care of it, so when it came back the next time, it will be more plentiful. They really controlled everything around them.... They remembered that when they took care of it, it would take care of them. So they really protected everything and tried to keep it producing more. They really did take care of it.

I remember we were told as youngsters that you never destroy plants around you, or trees around you, or rocks around you. They are alive. That is where you get your energy, from all these things around you. So you don't destroy all these things. That's what we were told. Now, when I see the non-Indians destroying everything around here, they are destroying all of us.

DD: So if there was some cataclysmic event tomorrow and we were all made homeless and had to live off the land, we couldn't exactly go back to the way things were?

AA: I don't think any of us could. Not even the Indians. You would have to know a whole lot more than what I am talking about right now.

DD: It wasn't just simple. It wasn't like the Garden of Eden—you just walked around and picked stuff?

AA: It only became the Garden of Eden if you had knowledge beforehand. But to go back suddenly, you would die. You would have to figure things out real quick. How are you going to catch a rabbit without a gun? What if you couldn't throw a rock straight? All the simple things you take for granted. It took some thinking to catch something, to hunt down a deer. You just didn't go up there and shoot it.

JM: I think land management meant management. Just that. You didn't let it lay. You went down and you

Well, I think the Cahuillas and other Indians were the first conservationists.

—*Anthony Andreas*

61

Cahuilla walk-in well, c. 1938

This crevice in the earth is a walk-in well, one of many dug by the desert Cahuilla as an ingenious solution to the problem of decreasing surface water. Southern California began a drying trend about five thousand years ago which will continue over the next five thousand years before completing the ten-thousand-year wet-dry cycle typical of lands in temperate latitudes.

Water resource management is an ancient skill, highly developed by the Cahuilla over time. Initially, walk-in wells may have been dug gradually as the water table lowered due to decreased snowpacks and rainfall. Paths were dug deeper and deeper to maintain access to the water. This practice also allowed animals in need of water to drink, thus assuring their continued presence.

The Romero expedition of 1823 first recorded the use of walk-in wells by the Cahuilla, some 120 feet deep. If you look carefully you can see a mustached man in cowboy's clothing and many stairs descending to the pool at the bottom of this well at Torres-Martinez, reportedly dug around 1828.

Photograph: C. C. Pierce
Collection of the Palm Springs Desert Museum

helped those things become productive. You watched them. You knew if there was insects that were going to take your food or whatever because of the drought, so you burned the stuff. Even if it looked wild and untouched, it was still being managed. It wasn't the border-to-border type of management. You know, your thinking was, like even my dad, if they went harvesting anything they never took it all. You didn't exhaust the supply to the point where you stripped everything.

DA: We set fires. Daddy said they set fires deliberately to control.

JM: Yeah, also when there was over-growth or if something was killing other stuff by overgrowing. So they managed that way. Even today, I think the whole thing is to make it productive. When my dad died, he wasn't there to manage the land he left us. How he managed it in his time was agriculture—the cattle and stuff. He always had a garden. Your yard was always cleaned and you would have your plants that were pretty, and you would have your plants that had a purpose.

Our aunts always did that, they always had, like a huge garden. They used to have bean fields. They used to have honey. So they always managed it. Today, you make it productive. Like we were saying, we did a lot of scarring with the excavation of the sand and gravel, but you just don't leave it. You manage it and you make it look pretty. Productiveness doesn't mean that it has to be actually utilized. It looks good.

DA: Basically, that is what JoMay and I are doing with our project. We kept a lot of acres set aside for mitigation and put it down where the children will have to keep it like that, the major parts of what we have. You don't exhaust the land. You use what will make you a living, but you don't have to over-build or over-dig. Sand and gravel is really lucrative, but we are really careful to make sure they stay within a perimeter, that there is a plan for after it has been used. Replanting is going to be done in phases. It is not going to stay looking like it is. It will even be a better place once you get it back into another state. I think people think of Indian people as exhausting

> Our aunts always did that, they always had a huge garden. They used to have bean fields. They used to have honey.
>
> —JoMay Modesto

63

The Land

I think they realized that . . . if you live close to the water you are going to conflict with each other.

—*JoMay Modesto*

the land to the point where you take everything out of it. You can't do that, because then it dies. It is not good for anybody or for anything.

JM: They thought about the water, too. I think they realized that first of all, if you live close to the water you are going to conflict with each other. You are going to contaminate the water source. You are going to disturb those animals that come to use the water. And then it wasn't healthy living around water—the dampness and stuff.

DA: It was just healthier to be away from it.

JM: Plus you contaminated your water source by living by it and you disturbed the animals that needed to come to use it.

AS: See, there is another thing—the water, the hot springs down there. Here in Palm Springs, it is different. Because it was right in the middle of the Cahuilla area, see? But you look at the one over in Warner's, that hot springs there. Before it was owned by the White, there, it was Cupeño, but everybody used it. The Diegueños came and used it, the Luiseños came and used it, the Cahuillas used it, the Cupeños used it. It didn't belong to anybody. It belonged to all of them.

DA: But look what the pioneers did. They built right

Measuring the Golsch Ditch, Flow 132.192", c. 1905
Early on, after having their traditional water sources stolen by government agents and settlers through the instrument of law which said anyone improving a water flow could claim exclusive rights to its use by filing a document for under $1.00, the Cahuilla learned to measure the flow so they could claim their own water. Water flow was measured by a standard measure called a "miner's inch," nine gallons per minute as measured through a four-inch pipe.
*Photograph: Charles F. Lummis
Collection of Southwest Museum, Los Angeles*

over the streams and springs and had it pumped right in there.

JM: I think the Cahuillas knew the dampness wasn't good for your physical being. When they chose where their house would be, I think they looked for a view. Not just a view, it was important to see who was coming, to be able to see what was going on around them, what was happening within their environment, if the enemy was coming or something was not right.

My own parents, they built the house where they had the best view, and we had to haul the water. Not only to wash dishes and drink water, but we had to haul water to water the plants. That's a lot of work. They had more of an eye on their environment, many people would do that. We had to climb a hill to do that and bring it back from the spring.

KS: I got a call the other day from some scientific company, where they have radio and electricity and things like that, and they said, "We see your report denying the crossing of that big power line on the Morongo Reservation." He said, "Did you write that letter after you read our book?" I said, "Are you kidding?" I was brought up there as a child with that, you know? "No," I said, "I never read

> But you look at the one over in Warner's, that hot springs there. Before it was owned by the White, there, it was Cupeño, but everybody used it.
>
> —*Alvino Siva*

A. B. Trott at contained well

The site of this well is Cavinish, a large Cahuilla community located in what is now called Indian Wells. It was deserted by the Cahuilla in the late 1900s, perhaps due to smallpox epidemics and the influx of non-Indian settlers.

The man seen here, A. B. Trott, proudly stands in front of this Cahuilla well capped for Anglo use. The capping of wells deprived Cahuilla people as well as local wildlife of access to the water, placing additional stress on the environment. Many wells were taken over by Anglos after the great epidemics of the 1860s wiped out entire villages.

Collection of the Palm Springs Historical Society

any book that you wrote. We were told when we were children to respect that power and so we don't want power close to our place, because it will kill you." And he said, "Oh I thought you read the book." [laughter] Did I read that book? [laughter] I said, "No, we know all about this."

JM: I think it goes back to what Alvino was saying, is that he is promoting this because he wants people to realize that there was power and respect and that there was intelligence, like in the creation story. I started thinking about it. When the twins created the earth and they couldn't make it stand up, so they put the axis in there, I thought, "These were dumb people?" [laughter] They didn't know. They

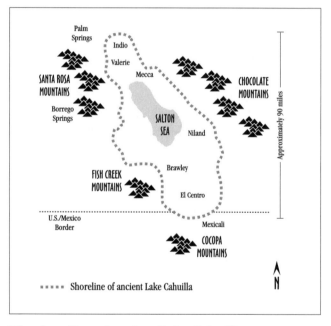

The shoreline of ancient Lake Cahuilla

This map shows the shoreline of ancient Lake Cahuilla, believed to have been created by overflow from the Colorado River much as the Salton Sea of today was formed in the last century. The shoreline of this ancient lake is dotted at suitable sites with the remains of ingeniously built rock fish traps, used to trick fish into thinking they were in the safety of a deep pool until it was too late and they were left stranded, unable to return to the body of the lake as its waters receded.

were more advanced than Europeans at that time. How did they know that they needed an axis?

AS: Fifty years ago, the Indian people started losing their interest in their tradition and their history and even their language, not even passing it on to their children. But when their children didn't learn the language, they didn't know the tradition, they didn't know their history, so they can't pass it on to the generation that is now.

Let me go back a little to what they used to tell us about my reservation when the Spanish was here. They used to try to tax the Indians and they would come onto my reservation and a lot of them were killed by Spaniards. And my dad used to tell me, "You see that high point there, that was where we used to see them, when the Spaniards were coming to collect." When they would see them coming, they would give the signal and then everybody would disappear. Nobody would be there when the Spaniards got there. After a while, they would leave them alone. But a lot of the Indian people were killed.

The younger generation don't know this. When they decided to put a dump on our reservation, the Indian people that didn't know their history—how the old people fought and died for that little 26,000 acres of land—said, "Yes, we would put a dump in there." Just because somebody came and said, "You will each get $5,000 a month." What is $5,000 a month compared to what is in that land? They don't know that. They don't have a clue. They just see that dollar sign… the heck with our generation. But we got together and we talked and we finally got it to where they could see that there was something there to hold onto.

What is $5,000 a month compared to what is in that land?

—*Alvino Siva*

Mojave Yucca

Courtesy of Palm Springs Desert Museum

FOOD & MEDICINE

KATHERINE SAUBEL: The Cahuillas used plants for food, for medicine, for housing, for clothing—for everything they used the plants, especially the medicine. A lot of the medicine that grows now, grows on the high hills. The ones that come from the mountains are the best medicine that can be used. That is why I fight so much to preserve all this, so we can continue and use these things. I still get my medicine plants from the mountains where I was born. That is why I would like to have it protected.

DA: I know how you make toys out of plants, dolls. [She begins the motions.] It was that thing that you would turn right over and it looks like she had a dress on and that was your doll. Have you ever done that JoMay? Where you pull the root out and make a doll? It was long and thin and you knot it for the head. The root comes out, about that long [she indicates about six inches].

JM: It was a ground cover. You pull it out and it has a long root. You turn it upside down and your ground cover is lacy, so it makes the dress. So the root makes the person. The root is thin, so you get the root and double it and make a couple of knots and you would have her head [laughter].

DD: Was there a strong ethnobotanic tradition in any of your families?

AA: Yeah, we drank the desert tea. I would go out with my grandmother when she wanted to pick some desert tea. There were different seasons when she picked barrel cactus. We didn't just go out and do it. When she went, I went, or we all went. We had mesquite trees growing right in our yard anyway. So when they bloomed, our grandmother would know they were good to eat. But she never prepared them, we just ate them off the tree. They had a kind of sweet taste to them.

DA: I had a bad experience with [medicinal plants]. That

> I still get my medicine plants from the mountains where I was born. That is why I would like to have it protected.
>
> —*Katherine Saubel*

ily—Mesquite Bean Pods
Prosopis juliflora var. *Torreyana*
Mesquite was a favored staple food of the Cahuilla. It was eaten fresh from the tree or dried and ground into meal which could be made into bread, porridge, or cakes.

Photograph: Steve Walag

was when I was young. I must have been about nine years old. I had impetigo all over my chin really bad. My cousins and I wanted to go to the show so bad. I wanted to go. I had like a poultice on. I remember all these leaves tied up with a rag. [She laughs, patting the underside of her chin.] And I go to this matinee on Sunday, in the afternoon. It was just all tied up here and there are sticks sticking out. People were looking at me [laughs]. I swore I was never going to do this again. Bobby and Gilbert were trying to walk in front of me. They were as embarrassed as I was [laughter].

One time we went out with my dad. We had some friends and stuff. He gave everybody a paper bag and told them to go get whatever they wanted to get. They came back and they dumped their bag of stuff in front of my dad and he would tell them what they got. We were surprised—wild tobacco, and this was used for this, and this is what we used this for. He used to say, "Out there is tons of food. Tons of food if you really look at it."

JM: I was fortunate, because when I married Marvin we moved to Santa Rosa [Reservation]. My kids were young. His aunt came to stay with his grandmother and she was really as traditional as you could get. She would get the girls and say, "Well, this is blooming, let's go pick some." She would make it fun. She would get the whole family out and we would go pick piñons. We would come home and we would dig a hole and put the fire in, and the next day clean them and stuff. She made it a lot of fun. She was really teaching us a lot. I am so thankful that we had that time with her.

AA: My grandmother used some medicine plants. I don't know what. She used to go pick some kind of herbs. We used to drink them. I remember she used to take me to her aunt. She lived in Coachella. She used to doctor me for stomach ailments. They would rub ashes on me and make me drink something. I don't know what it was. I never asked. Then too, we would go to a modern doctor. But a lot of times, she would take me to someone who was a medicine person.

KS: Well, my mother doctored with all the herbs and

> She would get the girls and say, "Well, this is blooming, let's go pick some."
>
> —JoMay Modesto, talking about her husband's aunt

71

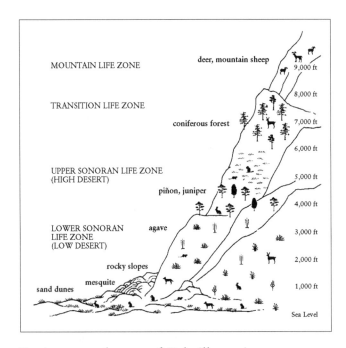

MOUNTAIN LIFE ZONE

deer, mountain sheep

9,000 ft

8,000 ft

TRANSITION LIFE ZONE

coniferous forest

7,000 ft

6,000 ft

UPPER SONORAN LIFE ZONE
(HIGH DESERT)

5,000 ft

piñon, juniper

4,000 ft

LOWER SONORAN
LIFE ZONE
(LOW DESERT)

agave

3,000 ft

2,000 ft

rocky slopes

mesquite

sand dunes

1,000 ft

Sea Level

Environmental zones of Cahuilla territory

The Cahuilla were roughly divided into three groups. Mountain Cahuilla clans occupied the Mountain and Transition life zones. Pass Cahuilla clans occupied the Upper Sonoran life zone. Desert Cahuilla clans occupied the Lower Sonoran life zone. All groups of the Cahuilla, however, visited the other life zones frequently. Close family ties throughout Cahuilla territory meant regular trips to visit and trade with other clans. Katherine Saubel remembers that at Los Coyotes, a Mountain life zone community, several families would temporarily relocate to the desert to escape the cold winters. Chief Patencio, from a Lower Sonoran life zone clan, recounts regularly spending summers in the mountains.

Adapted from chart by Gary Tong from The Cahuilla, *by Lowell J. Bean and Lisa Bourgeault*

things like that. That's why I remember so much about it. When we were growing up, we never went to the doctor. She doctored us. If it was something more serious than that, well the shamans were still alive, and they would doctor us. We never went to the doctor at all.

They treated everything, whatever happened to you. I remember when my brother got sick one time. He was maybe just about four years old, and he would sit outside and play around on the ground. You know how babies always put something in their mouth—well, he was eating the sand. It was all sand in Palm Springs. He had cramps and his stomach was hurting him, so my mother called the old man, Pedro Chino, and he came over and doctored him. He said his stomach was knotted up because he had so much sand in it. He fixed that. He told them what was happening, he took that pain away. My brother was all right, but Pedro Chino said, "Watch him, that he doesn't eat more of that. A little bit wouldn't hurt. But all the time, well then you aren't watching him." He doctored him and he was fine. They also had women that were really doctors by different methods that they used themselves.

AA: I was told everything was in the mind, by the medicine man. He said it was all up here, but people make it something. That is why they would have to have ceremonies. The ceremony helped ease people's minds. If you told them that they didn't need that, the people wouldn't know what to do. Other cultures have that too. A person can will themselves to die without any cause. Like getting bewitched, they know they are going to die. They will die without any cause, because of that belief.

Not to say that this is witchcraft. I am not making light of it. It did happen. It is all from the mind. You have to remember, before the Europeans came and there were conveniences or modern tools, all the Indians had were their minds. That's all they had. They had no tools... well, they had little stone tools. But other than that, they had to survive with only their minds. I think their mind was much more superior to our minds today for problem solving.

DD: We have it so easy, we can be so lazy.

> Before the Europeans came and there were conveniences or modern tools, all the Indians had were their minds.
>
> —*Anthony Andreas*

73

qexe'yily—Prickly pear cactus

Opuntia occidentalis
At least three varieties of prickly-pear cactus can be found in Cahuilla territory. In traditional times all these varieties were probably eaten. The edible fruit is ready for harvesting between May and August, depending on the elevation. The joints can also be diced and eaten.

Photograph: Steve Walag

AA: You just have to turn on the TV and get all the information you want. You don't even have to think, "Uh, is this the right button—on or off?" That's all we have to do. If you train your fingers to do that for you, you don't even have to think. It is just reflex. They knew about the stars, they knew about the world. Deep, deep things. Psychiatrists and psychologists are just finding out now. One doctor told me, when we were talking about witchcraft and medicine-man healing, he said there is a lot of things medical science don't know yet about healing. A modern doctor told me that.

DA: One thing here is different ways of knowing. There is the kind of Western scientific way of knowing and then there is the Cahuilla way of knowing. The same thing with this medicine thing and the shamans. Here was this wisdom, and western science says, "No, it is wrong. It can't be verified." And this criteria of knowing, they have gradually come closer to recognizing that they didn't know it all. They thought they knew it all, and they didn't know it all.

KS: You know why? It is because they thought we were just imbeciles. We didn't think when they first got here that is the way they looked at us. But we weren't imbeciles. We had everything with us. But they didn't want to learn from us. Now they are finding out.

DD: How many people still know how to fix an herbal remedy?

AS: Not many. There is a lot of plants that I know of that the people use, but I don't know what it looks like. I am going to have to go down there to Sat Torres. He knows a little bit about those medicines down there. I am going to have to go down there and see how it is done.

Here, in 1967, '68, my brother, he was still living then in his place up at Los Coyotes, he had a fenced-in property. It must have been about eighty or ninety acres, a huge place which needed fencing. Anyway, he got this old guy, his name was Joe, to help me. He was a Mexican fellow in his late fifties. We fenced it, the Mexican and myself. Just when we were about to finish, my brother bought a little house trailer for the Mexican to live in by his place. So one morning that Mexican didn't show up. He was sick. He had diarrhea real bad. We don't know what caused it. Something he ate or water or whatever. Montezuma just caught up with him. He was getting weak and couldn't get out. My brother was worried. So my brother had this medicine, he said, "Well, what I am going to try is our herbs, our medicine, and see what it does." I go with him to pick this. I am looking at something else up there on the side of this hill. So he goes over to one side and I go over the other side, then he comes back with a bundle of leaves. I didn't say, "Let me take a look at them, what bush did you get them from?" I didn't ask him that. He put them in a little sack and went back. He brewed that for that Mexican guy and it stopped that diarrhea just like that. I went over there and I tried to look at the plants where he picked that. They all looked the same to me. I don't know which ones he took.

They knew about the stars, they knew about the world. Deep, deep things.

—Anthony Andreas

75

We used those foods during the Second World War, on account of a lot of things were closed to us.... But I think it was really nice for us, because we went back to our own food, like the acorn, the mesquite, and the different things we used to live on.

—Katherine Saubel

KS: Well, most of that is gone. The areas where we gathered for food or gathered for plants are now occupied by other than Indians. We don't have a right to that anymore. Of course, then a lot of them have used it for range, for cattle and horses. The animals eat a lot of this food that we ate. There is really nothing there for us anymore. Only in our own reservations if it still grows there. That is why I would like to have the reservations kept from being destroyed. That is where we get our medicine, our food, everything, from the mountainside. Those areas that have all these trees and things that we use should be kept alive and not be destroyed. Otherwise, we won't have anywhere to get anything—for food, for anything.

DD: How old were you when these traditional foods and medicines went out of daily use?

AA: Traditional. Do you mean beans and tortillas?

DD: I mean barrel cactus and mesquite.

AA: I must have been about twelve or thirteen.

DD: Do you ever eat those foods now, other than when you get together?

AA: That's the only time we eat it now. Acorns and other Indian foods. Mostly during ceremonies.

DD: Then you get *sawish* and *wewish* [traditional tortillas and acorn-meal porridge]?

AA: Well, we eat tortillas all the time. Wewish only at functions. At birthday parties we will have foods like that too.

DD: I had my first barrel cactus last year. It is so good.

AA: It is good, huh? There used to be some barrel cactus close to where we used to live, but they are no longer there. A lot of people would come and get them for landscaping. They are doing that now. There weren't that many anyway. But there is none there now. It was about a mile from our house. There are still some way back in the Palm Canyon area. There are a lot of them. But we never climbed, we just went to the closest.

KS: We used those foods during the Second World War, on account of a lot of things were closed to us. You couldn't buy that, you had to have a stamp for this, you had to do this. But I think it was really nice for us, because we went back to our own food, like the acorn, the mesquite, and the different things we used to live on. That was our supplement. We didn't have to depend on buying at the store. We went back to our own food, like the barrel cactus and the yucca blossoms, everything. We ate all that again. We weren't really hungry during the Depression. I was raised during the Depression.

I don't think the young people care much about getting a good diet anymore at all, because they can run up to McDonald's or wherever now. It is not very good, but that is where they go now. It is less work, I suppose, but that is not very good either. I have always thought about that too—they didn't have any high cholesterol because they didn't eat anything fat. When they had to cook something, they either boiled it or just cooked it over the fire. A lot of these animals that are out in the fields— like the deer, they don't have high cholesterol. Now we have pork chops, bacon, and things like that. That's why the change was.

DD: Will you tell about the first introduction of bacon to the Cahuilla?

KS: Yes [laughs]. My mother was telling me about her mother and the people down in the desert. They sent one of those slabs of bacon to the Indian people. They never saw bacon before in their lives and they didn't know what to do with it, so they heated with it. They would put it over the fire and boy, it burnt. They just loved it. They used it as wood [laughter]. It was really something, I guess.

There was another thing that really surprised me. My grandmother was telling me—she lived with us until she died, she was one of my great teachers, my mentor—and she said the government gave them their first boxes of fruit, fresh figs. They sent figs to them. They told them it was good to eat. "You eat them." They should have said, "You eat it like this." Because when they broke them open, the inside looked like worms. "Oh," they said, "it's wormy." They threw them all away. They thought they were all wormy. They never ate them because they never saw a fig before [laughs]. Gee, I love figs, and they threw them all away [laughter]. Oh gosh.

> They sent one of those slabs of bacon to the Indian people. They never saw bacon before in their lives and they didn't know what to do with it, so they heated with it.... They used it as wood.
>
> —*Katherine Saubel*

Panu'ul—Our Lord's Candle, Spanish Bayonet

Yucca whipplei

Stems of yucca plants were harvested both before and after blooming, and roasted in three-foot-deep parabolic pits lined with heated rocks and sealed over with rock and sand. Before blooming, the stems are sometimes called "hearts," and are prepared by removing the spine-tipped leaves before roasting. The flower stalks are harvested when they are three or four feet tall, before they become too tough and stringy to be palatable. They are fibrous and chewed like sugar cane to extract the sweet juice. Some stems are spared so the plants can bloom, and likewise, some blossoms are spared so the sweet seed pods can be harvested in summer.

Photograph: Steve Walag

JM: I was reading an article in *Cosmopolitan* and they were talking in the "Dieter's Notebook" about Indian food being so high in fiber. Maybe we need to go back to that. There is so much there. I can remember when we had gone out and worked on the Cahuilla workshops.* We had done the cooking. One of the things that we took was elderberry tea, and everybody went crazy over it. I think, this tea is so good, why don't we drink it more often? We just did it that year because they want to try and go back to native food as much as possible. Piñon, all kinds of stuff that is out there. We know what a little bit of it is, but we don't utilize it as much as we should in our everyday diet. If we did, we would have less diabetes and I am sure less cancer and less heart problems.

DD: You told me, a long time ago, I think, that sometimes you still gather—your nieces and nephews and cousins and you gather piñon.

JM: We have gone collecting, just to do it.

DD: Well, would you go through the process for preparing piñon in the traditional way? How you would do it today?

JM: Okay. They had in Santa Rosa the piñons, the pine-nut trees. You would knock the cones down. You would have a long pole and it would take you all day. You would get all dirty and sappy. Then, while they are still closed, before they actually opened up, you make a fire and dig a hole and then put the coals in the hole and put a layer of dirt on them. Then you put the cones in there and cover them up and let them roast overnight so they just naturally roast and burst open. Then you would have to clean them. Then you would get really dirty.

DD: How do you clean them?

JM: You squash the pine cone—almost like shelling walnuts. When you would squash them, like with a rock, they would open up and then you would be able to shake out the seeds. Then you would put the seeds in a basket.

DD: And the seeds come in a little husk themselves?

JM: In a little shell. They are little, tiny, round... they

> Piñon, all kinds of stuff that is out there... we don't utilize it as much as we should in our everyday diet. If we did, we would have less diabetes and I am sure less cancer and less heart problems.
> —JoMay Modesto

---

* Workshops in traditional skills offered to the public.

79

Panu'ul—Our Lord's Candle, Spanish Bayonet (detail)

Yucca whipplei

Many pounds of yucca flowers were picked by the women each spring. Like the roasted hearts and flower stalks of yucca, some of the flowers were eaten fresh, but most were dried and stored for future use. In this way yucca was a major source of fresh food for four or five months in the spring and summer. In the remaining months of the year, dried yucca products were rehydrated for use. Mrs. Saubel uses modern equipment to preserve the blossoms, much as a farm wife cans green beans to preserve them.

Photograph: Steve Walag

are like raisins maybe, but smooth. They are actually little tits [laughter]. That's what they look like when they are all blown up. They fall out of the cone that is open. You put them in the tray, the basket, and you winnow them, you throw them up in the air. The wind takes what you don't need away. Then you eat them.

DD: With the shell on?

JM: No, you have to crack the shell. Just bite into it. Because they are about the size of maybe a pea, maybe a little bigger. You just bite into them and then you have the pine nut in there. It is almost like an almond.

DD: So if a woman wanted to prepare a dish that was largely made up of pine nuts, she would crack each one with her teeth and shell them?

JM: Uh huh… they are so small. So you just crack them and open them up. Kenny brought down a bunch of really big ones from Las Vegas. He had already had them out of the cone, but they weren't roasted. I guess they opened them up and took them out before they were roasted. He brought them and they weren't roasted, but they were really big. What I did, I put them in my microwave and roasted them in the microwave and dried them out. You just keep turning them. We only put them on for maybe five minutes. Well, my microwave isn't really what you would call high, intense. It is kind of low, so that it takes longer. But that is how we did it. You don't salt them or nothing. It has a really distinctive taste. Boy, we ate them all.

DA: I know there was one thing that I used to chew for toothaches. I don't know what it was. That is what was sad. I know the kids used to make their own gum, Daddy showed them how. They probably know more than I do because Daddy took the time, I guess, to show them. But they know how to do that gum. How to cook it and put it on the back of the stove, and then it is supposed to clean your teeth. I don't know what it is. It is some kind of plant.

JM: It gets all gummy—sappy—when it coagulates.

I know my cousin hated chia [*Salvia columbariae*]. They used to cook it with Cream of Wheat. He said it was awful, he didn't like it at all.

I know the kids used to make their own gum, Daddy showed them how…. How to cook it and put it on the back of the stove, and then it is supposed to clean your teeth.

—*Dolores Alvarez*

81

There was a plant down in Soboba that grows in the river.... They would boil it and wash their hair in it. It would keep you from going gray, but you don't have dyed hair.

—Dolores Alvarez

DA: There was a plant down in Soboba that grows in the river. Lena Rhodes took me out to show me. They would boil it and wash their hair in it. It would keep you from going gray, but you don't have dyed hair.

AS: We know about that thing for abortion. But I would hate to brew it for somebody and then something happens—a woman dies or girl dies and it's your fault. The old people years ago probably knew another remedy for whatever happened that caused it, the antidote, which I don't know.

And then there is another thing, but I haven't had anybody yet to try it out on, but they say it is real good. But it is for piles, hemorrhoids. And they say that it cured people that had it really bad. This one cowboy was telling me that he knew what I was talking about. He said, "I have used it." He was working at Warner's Ranch. He said, "It got so bad, I was bleeding so bad that I had to put a pillow on my saddle so I could work and ride. It was that bad."

What it is, there are so many varieties of oak. This one variety, you take the bark off it. Between the bark and the tree itself, I don't know how you would explain it... you have a little fiber. You take that fiber and you boil it. You just dip a piece of cotton in there and put it up there. He said that thing will just draw it out. In one day, he said. He said, "I threw that pillow away the next day."

JM: I know there are a couple of things, what do you call it? It's a root and you make a solution out of it. It was to cleanse, an antiseptic. If you had a sore you would clean it with that.

I still cook a lot of yucca. I usually do that when it comes out.

DA: JoMay's is good. JoMay cooked when we went to the [Cahuilla workshop] with Tom Fresh. We had a fire made as big as this [she indicates the four-foot tabletop] in the ground. We served thirty people everything. We cooked a whole meal outside. We didn't have rabbit, we used chicken. And we made fry bread, tortillas, beans, yucca, stew.

JM: The [yucca] blossoms come out in about late May, depending on the rain and the warmth. When they blossom, you just cut it, the whole stalk and everything. If the blossoms are closed you just pick them. You have to boil them. But if they are opened and they have a little yellow stem, you take the stem out because that is the bitter part. The real, real bitter part. And then you boil it. You boil it about maybe two or three times, I guess leach it. It depends on how bitter they are. Then it almost becomes like a cabbage. Then you can prepare it. A lot of people will cook it with, like eggs, scrambled eggs. What I like to use is bacon. Fry up bacon and cut it up and then add that yucca to it. It has a really good flavor.

DA: You did the stalk once.

JM: Yeah, the stalk. You can take the stalk and cut it up. We wrapped it in foil and put it right into the coals of the fire. The stem has to be fresh. They are usually about this big [she makes a circle with her fingers as big as a half-dollar]. It has to be a special yucca. It has to be the kind, I don't know what they call them, the candlestick ones. We have a lot of them.

DD: And they grow really tall?

JM: I am talking about the kind that are spindled like this [she indicates a tall, thin stalk]. Well, the stem comes up. The base just shoots the big flower stalk up. It has real narrow leaves that are in a clump at the bottom. So you can take the stalk and then we just cut them up into three or four-inch pieces and wrap them up in foil and roast it on the coals overnight. Then you eat them. It is almost like a sweet potato. It is really good. My dad loved them. It is good.

A lot of people will cook [yucca] with... scrambled eggs. What I like to use is bacon. Fry up bacon and cut it up and then add that yucca to it. It has a really good flavor.

—JoMay Modesto

Alvino Siva, 1990

In traditional times, young men and boys of the Cahuilla community apprenticed themselves to a teacher in order to learn the hundreds of bird songs. A precise dose of a concoction of the potentially deadly but sacred datura was given to young boys as a memory aid. This is not practiced in modern times because there are no more Cahuilla shamans who can prepare the datura.

Photograph: John Bishop

BIRD SONGS

ANTHONY ANDREAS: A lot was written about the creation songs and the other songs, deer songs, whatever. But they didn't survive, I think, because they were ritual. Bird singing has survived longer than our other traditions. I think the reason why it survived—not so much of it was mentioned in the early writings of the anthropologists—is because anybody could sing the bird songs.

Only certain persons could sing the ritual songs. The bird songs—well, if you were interested in bird songs, you could learn. You didn't have to be chosen. You had to have the desire.

When I was growing up I said, "I would like to sing those songs," but I never thought in my wildest dreams that I would be singing them. I just wanted to be a part of it. I wanted to sing with Joe Patencio and Bert Levi, be a part of it, never thinking they would die. I was an adult already, but before I was thirty. I never thought beyond that, that I would be singing. There was a lot of singers, they have all died.

DD: What is a bird singer?

AA: Well, what is a bird singer? It is a person who sings bird songs. Anybody could be a bird singer. Some know more than others. I have seen guys when I was growing up, early twenties, late teens, they would argue about a certain song. They would get into arguments about similar songs. One would sing it different than the other. They would both accuse each other of singing it wrong. "My grandfather taught it to me like this." "My father taught it to me this way, he was a bird singer and he knew all the songs." "Well, so did my grandfather," and so on. I used to ask them why they were arguing. I couldn't figure it out. Maybe it was the drinks or something.

But I learned later on, Joe Patencio told me, no

I made my own little rattle out of a milk can and would sit in there. My mother would say, "Get away, you are throwing them off...."
But they would tell her, "No, leave him alone. That is the way he is going to learn."

—*Alvino Siva*

85

Bird Songs

From what I understand, these are social songs sung at a time where lineages or the tribes get together for a festive occasion.

—*Anthony Andreas*

matter how a person sings the songs, they are both right. It is how they learned it. If you are singing these songs, well, whoever is going to sing with you will sing it your way. When you sing with them, you are going to sing it their way. It is so simple. Nobody is wrong and everybody is right. It is how they learned it. I have heard so many criticisms— "You don't know to sing it, you don't sing them right." Well, what is the right way? That is how I learned them.

DD: How did bird singing begin?

AS: Well, before I go into how it started, I will start with how I got into it. They had bird singing at the time in Palm Springs at the ceremonial house, but I don't remember going. My mother probably would have taken me, but I don't remember being there. But every summer, after school, we would come up here, move to Morongo or move over here to Banning. My father would work on the fruit and my mother would work in the fruit shed. So this one year we came. I think I was six years old, five or six, because I wasn't in school yet. We were over there at the Gilman Ranch and there was a regular Indian village. There were Indians from all over. Not only Cahuillas—Luiseño Indians, everybody.

Everybody was there. They were all working in the fruit. Every Friday night, somebody would start singing bird songs. It was about five different bird singers and each one of them had a different style of bird singing. It was all the same, it was just different clans, I guess—I can't describe it. But I know there was a guy by the name of Martin, he sang the songs. Then there was a guy by the name of Garcia, Chris Garcia, he would sing. And there was another, two, three more singers that would sing. Well, Friday evening at about six, they would get together and start singing. This is how I got hooked on it. I would go over there and listen. Then I started dancing and singing with them. I got to the point where I would make my own little rattle. They all had their own rattles. I made my own little rattle out of a milk can and would sit in there. My mother would say, "Get away, you are throwing them off," because I didn't know, see. But they would tell her,

"No, leave him alone. That is the way he is going to learn." I finally picked it up.

Oh, I guess I was about seven then, six, seven years old. But I started over here. Joe Patencio, I knew him. When I was about seven I think Joe was about twelve or thirteen already. We would play together, because I was big for my age. Then we started singing. I would go to his house and we would sing the bird songs laying in bed. A lot of times, we would make mistakes. Joe's father was a singer. He would laugh and he would correct us. That was clear on up until I went into the service, I was singing with Joe. Joe wasn't a head singer yet, when I left for the service at about twenty. They had the older singers still alive.

See, when you become a singer, you don't just say, "I am going to sing this song." You tell the people—you feed the people—then you say, "Okay, I am going to sing. This is going to be my song." Then you sing, whether it is bird songs or a ceremonial song. Whenever you have to come out, they would say, "You are coming out," see? You don't have that anymore, it is all gone.

AA: From what I understand, these are social songs sung at a time where lineages or the tribes get together for a festive occasion, for whatever reason.

And this was about the only time that the women could join in and really be part of it—let their hair down, so to speak. Most of the other rituals were all handled by men. This was the time too that women could make fun of the men. Tease them if they made a mistake in their dance step or in the song. I remember some of them, they are passed on now, they used to tease me too, when I first started singing by myself. It was very frightening. When Joe Patencio and Bert Levi were still alive, I could sing with them. When they died, everybody expected me to sing. I didn't think I was going to sing, until I was encouraged to sing. They were told by Joe Patencio to help that young boy. I was already thirty. That was young to them, I suppose. So I started singing.

If I made a mistake, the women would laugh right away. It was just fun. A lot of guys didn't like

87

I think criticism is a sincere form of flattery. I used to get a lot of criticism.

—*Anthony Andreas*

criticism. They'd say, "Oh, I'm not going to dance tomorrow, I'm not going to sing tomorrow." "How come?" "Well, they made fun of me." That's all part of it. If you can't take criticism from women, then you had no business being there. Right? And a lot of women helped me, too. I think criticism is a sincere form of flattery. I used to get a lot of criticism.

I don't get so much teasing anymore because most of my audience is younger. I used to get teasing from the older ones, who are passing on now. There is only a few left now. There is Laura Holmes. She keeps me in place.

AS: Then when I got into these songs, I wanted to know how it originated, how the songs came about. So this old man, Mariano, that is Joe Patencio's father, he wouldn't really just sit down and tell us everything and how it was kept and whatever, he just said our bird songs started way back with our creation stories.

When they killed Mukat, everybody was in turmoil, everybody just went their ways. When you hear about the creation I think it was nothing but Cahuillas, but everybody else was there. Everything that Mukat had created. So when he died, they just dispersed. They went to the four winds. What Cahuillas were left, they said, "Let us look around and listen to the people that are talking Cahuilla and let's get them together, let's get our people together. So they did that, they got all the Cahuillas together. They said they went around this continent three times. These songs they sang, these bird songs. That is why the songs are so ancient you can't understand them. Some of them you can understand. Some of the songs are singing about the land, and it parallels the migration of the birds a little bit too. The songs are not only about birds, you have the animals in them. He said, "This is what we sang when we landed here in that area, Palm Springs." That is where those songs came from I guess, from when they were moving. The songs can be sad or they can be joyous, you know. It tells us of the movement of the people, actually, but it sounds like the movement of the birds. They compare it to the birds, that is why they are using bird names in there.

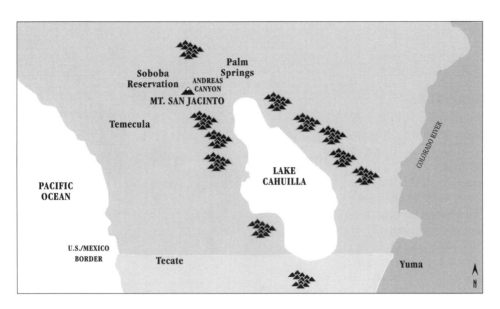

AA: It is my understanding that the migration started in Palm Springs, after the death of the creator, Mukat. According to what I was told and understand, the people got sad and confused. They didn't know what to do. They went to look for another place to live. It was a terrible thing they did, causing Mukat's death. So they went southeast to Yuma. That's why a lot of the songs, I think, are in that language. Maybe they traded songs, too. What I understand, from what Joe Patencio said, there was some songs we sang in the Yuma language. Then we went down into Mexico and, of course, there was a lot of hardship. It was a harsh land, a lot of desert. I think they decided to come back. Where they originated from was the best place of all. But they didn't come back by the same route. In fact, they went towards Tecate and through Temecula and through this way. Then once we got close to home, through Soboba. We were so anxious to get home that we flew over the San Jacinto Mountains. There is a hill at the mouth of the Andreas Canyon where my clan landed. Joe Patencio's clan kept going and they skated by the spa and caused the water to come up. Well, that's what he told me. Now whether he was making it up or not—I didn't ask him if it was true or not. He told me that, and it sounded good to me. How the other clans arrived, I don't know. Some

Bird song map

Shown here are some of the places mentioned by Anthony Andreas as being part of the migrations that inspired the bird songs.

89

Robert Levi, 1990

In the late 1980s the bird singers received a Master/Apprentice grant from the California Arts Council. Here, Torres-Martinez singer Robert Levi sings bird songs with apprentices Mark Macarro and Luke Madrigal, two of a new generation of young men who are dedicated to preserving the art, known affectionately as "singing birds."

Photograph: John Bishop

say they came through the pass here from Soboba this way.

DD: So the bird songs are specifically about the migration, about the route, about the time, or their adventures on the way?

AA: Well, I don't understand all the songs. I just know the story behind those songs. That's what I told you. There are certain things that happened on the way that is recorded in these songs. The different people they meet on the way, but they are birds. They are different birds. In the songs, they become birds. There is this other song, the return song. "The ground is beautiful because they are coming closer to the home. They are recognizing their home place." That is why they fly over. They are so anxious to get home, they fly over the San Jacinto Mountains.

DD: And being birds, that is not so hard.

AA: That is right. When I was growing up, I didn't know that story. They used to call them "birds." That's how we grew up. I didn't ask why they called them birds. No one asked that. Then when Joe Patencio told me this story, it kind of made sense. My grandmother didn't tell me much, but that it was a journey. They never went into what specific things they did or... But Joe Patencio went a little farther and said we went to Yuma and met those people there. But they were birds in the songs.

DD: Now other Cahuilla versions of the migration include travels all the way down into South America and over to New England and...

AA: Oh yeah. Well, I don't know. After the death of Mukat it could very well be that others have taken off from this very same migration and went farther. Maybe these particular people didn't go as far. I can't say.

There is this other song, the return song. "The ground is beautiful because they are coming closer to the home. They are recognizing their home place."

—*Anthony Andreas*

Rattles from the old days

The use of a gourd as a sound chamber for a rattle is common, but a host of other materials have been used as well. In this photo you can see a rattle inspired by designs from prehistory. A small tortoise shell has been wrapped with copper wire to create a fabric in the spaces where the tortoise's head and other appendages protruded. A stick has been worked and added as a handle. In the old days, plant fibers or leather thongs were used to make the fabric element of the rattle. The 20th century offered another favorite material for rattles, evaporated milk cans. Anthony Andreas and Alvino Siva both remember finding milk cans as children and making rattles much like the one shown here.

Photograph: Deborah Dozier

Bird Songs

Saturnino Torres at age 76, 1990

Born in 1913, noted Cahuilla elder from Torres-Martinez Saturnino Torres has a message for Cahuilla children:
"Work hard. Keep away from drugs. Try and learn as much as you can about our culture. Don't let it die completely."

Photograph: John Bishop

Bird Singers, 1990

Boys begin their bird-singing apprenticeship while very young, learning the bird songs little by little, taking a more prominent role in the group as their skills and technique improve. In bird singing, as in most other aspects of Cahuilla culture, the eldest bird singer in the group is the lead singer. Each geographic area has its own group of bird singers. The most prominent elder bird singers are Saturnino Torres, Robert Levi, Alvino Siva, and Anthony Andreas. This group of bird singers at the Malki Fiesta features (left to right) guest singer Paul Apodaca, Ernie Siva, Mark Macarro, Alvino Siva, Saturnino Torres, and Luke Madrigal.

Collection of Malki Museum

And all these migrations could have been at the same time, is what I'm telling you. But this is the only part that I know of. I'm not saying that is it, maybe there was more in between that we have forgotten. Maybe these bird songs are the ones we know now, it could be the tail end of the journey. I can't say.

DD: Tony, how long have you been singing on your own?

AA: Since '75, 1975.

DD: What is the future of bird singing?

AS: At first, Will Austin, Joe Patencio, and I said, "Hey, we are going to be losing these songs. We have to do something." So I started continuing the singing. I sang by myself at the Malki Museum for about, I guess, three years. And then I got my nephew Robert Levi into it. His father was a singer. He didn't really follow it. He didn't sit with his father and learn all the songs. His father's songs are a little different than Joe Patencio's songs. Anyway, so, I got him to go and then somebody—I think it was Paul Apodaca—said, "You people can get a grant given to you for teaching apprentices." So Robert said, "Let's see if we can get us some boys." So we got three or four boys and we got a grant. But what I am running into now, you know, it does—well it does take many years to become a singer. You don't become a singer just overnight. You can't say, "I know these songs."

DD: Have you taught a lot of singers, too?

AA: Well, I don't exactly teach them. If they want to sing, they listen. I have never sat down and taught anybody.

DD: So it is not a formal education process?

AA: No. I should, but I don't. They just learn it by listening to me. Some boys have learned since they were this high. Now they are adult, 25 years old.

DD: Does someone have to be invited to sing or can they just come out of a desire to sing?

AA: They just sit down sometimes, hey, they are here.

DD: You start with kids that are two or three years old?

AA: Yeah. At 18 they are over the hill, especially the girls. I have two boys who were young. Now they are in their twenties and they sing with me.

AS: I remember this old man, Perfecto Segundo, would

It does take many years to become a singer. You don't become a singer just overnight. You can't say, "I know these songs."

—*Alvino Siva*

Kiksawva'al (Jimsonweed, Thorn-Apple)
Datura meteloides

This deadly beauty is well respected by the elders as the source of a powerful drug used in prehistoric and historic times during the transition from boyhood to manhood. The recipe for extracting the drug is no longer known. Elders sadly shake their heads and relate the stories of young people who didn't understand the power hidden in each part of the plant and died experimenting with it.

According to Alvino Siva, after the shamans had prepared the potion which caused hallucinations, disorientation, and paralysis they administered only one drop to the initiates who were to participate in the ceremony. It was used as a memory aid for the boys who had to learn large amounts of material during the ceremonial period.

Photograph: Deborah Dozier

say that when they were teaching the kids the songs, they would give them this dream weed, Jimson. They would put it in their cups and the kids would get drunk and then they sing the songs to them. There must be something in there that works on your memory so the kids won't forget the songs. I might do that, try that myself. But they said just a little bit. When you brew it, just put your finger in it and then put it on the tongue. That is enough right there. Don't drink it.

DD: I know many Indian and non-Indian kids have died from trying to use that plant.

AS: Oh yeah, because they don't know what it is all about.

DD: Isn't the bird the major hero or another animal is the major hero talking about how to overcome difficulty, how to overcome adversity? This was a method of passing down what? Physics, chemistry…

AS: And history.

DD: And cosmology…

AS: Yes, they sing about the stars, they sing about the seven sisters. They sing about the spider that is supposed to be in the stars. The spider is a tarantula. This one portion where it says, "They are climbing, those seven sisters. They are climbing." Then, "They are leaving, they are going." The one that follows is telling, "They have climbed. They are gone, they are there now."

And then the next one says, this is towards the morning, the song says, "These are the ones, the first that he had put there." Up there, it says, there is a blue streak that is the seven sisters. There is a blue dot and that is the spiders. That is what the song is about. But a lot of them now want to interpret it different, but I am just interpreting it by what the old people say to me. So I go by what they always told. Now Tony's songs, I don't know what his songs are about. His are altogether different. Anyway, they supposedly started that way from years back, millions of years back, I guess, from as long as we have been here.

These were just for joyous occasions. But they had different songs for a death. Then afterwards you can sing bird songs.

> Yes, they sing about the stars, they sing about the seven sisters. They sing about the spider that is supposed to be in the stars. The spider is a tarantula.
>
> —*Alvino Siva*

Cahuilla bird singers and bird dancers, c. 1990
This is Anthony Andreas' group of bird singers and
dancers from the Painiktum clan. Everyone is invited to
join in this dance.
Photograph: George Piquino
Collection of the Malki Museum

DD: Which is why there is the restraint against singing bird songs for a year after a death?

AS: Yes. This is a restriction against you singing if someone in your family has died. Close family, maybe like my brother or my sister. Then you don't sing for a year.

DD: How many bird songs are there?

AS: When I came back from out of the service and we would be singing together, Joe would say to me, "What is next?" I would think and I would think, "This is next," and I would sing him the song and he would say, "No. That is another group." He would tell me there are three groups of those songs. Who knows how many songs?

You can sing from seven o'clock in the evening until six or seven o'clock in the morning and just take maybe a half-hour or forty-five-minute break at midnight for coffee—to get coffee and pie, whatever, you know. And you sing one song for maybe three, four minutes. That is a lot of songs.

How you can keep those songs in sequence is the big question. How can you remember that this comes and then this one next, see?

I can probably sing maybe four or five hours now, but then I am kind of… Nobody else knows either whether I am singing in the right sequence. If they ask me to sing and I listen to my recordings, the main one I got is a tape with just a few words of the song. On my little cassette like that, I have to plug it in my ear and I will push the button and it will play the beginning of each one of them. I never counted how many songs I have.

AA: You learn just by memory. To the old songs there is no meaning. I mean the meaning has been forgotten. But they go with a story. A story about the migration. These songs were taught to those singers. A certain part of the series. It is all in category. There is a pattern and a system to all these songs.

DD: So you have to go in the proper sequence?

AA: Yeah.

DD: And if you get out of the proper sequence, do you have to back up to where you were doing it right and go again?

AA: No. Maybe that was done before, but I know Joe

> You can sing from seven o'clock in the evening until six or seven o'clock in the morning.... And you sing one song for maybe three, four minutes. That is a lot of songs.
>
> —*Alvino Siva*

Cahuilla Women Dancers, 1976

These women are dancing at the Andreas Ranch in Andreas Canyon, traditional home of the Painiktum clan. The women are from the Agua Caliente Band of Cahuilla Indians. Beautiful ribbon dresses were adopted by the women at Agua Caliente in the 1900s. The tradition was abandoned by the 1930s but recently they have again become fashionable.

Back: Eugene Segundo, Jr.

Center (left to right): Lois Segundo Lewis, Annette Segundo Guzman, Cindy St. John, Michelle Andreas

Front: Paula Andreas, Anna Patencio, Ronette Saubel, Lorena Saubel, Leila Saubel

Collection of the Malki Museum

Patencio used to skip around. He would start off with a certain series, and then after a while, he would just skip around.

DD: How do you keep all this knowledge recorded?

AA: I got a little crank here... [He points to the side of his head.]

DD: You have memorized the sequences and all the words...

AA: Just the beginning parts. After the first couple of hours, I just skip around too. If you sing one song, you have to be thinking about the next two, what's the next two. They almost sound alike. Sometimes I can't remember the next one, so I go to the one after that. Later, if I want to, I come back and pick that one up after a break. I gotta take a ten-minute break. I usually sing anywhere from a couple of hours to all night.

I have taped five one-hour tapes. But I don't sing them all. I have these written down. My grandmother had a book. A lot of those... the only thing is that I remember the tune. So I would look at these words that she wrote. Pretty soon I would get the tune. As I was growing up, I would do that. I got this book in the early sixties. I was always trying to figure out what the songs were. I got about half of them figured out. With the help of Joe Patencio, I learned a lot of songs that I never sang before. I had heard them, so it was easier to pick them up.

DD: So did your grandmother write down the whole song, or just the first line?

AA: The first line, because if you wrote the whole song it would take a whole page. So she would write just the first line. You sing each line three times.

DD: So there is a formal structure for these songs?

AA: Yes. And you have to remember it too. Sometimes I will forget. You sing that verse three times, and you go up high twice, then you do it again three more times, go up high twice, then three more times, then after the last two you quit.

DD: So for each song there is one phrase, and you repeat it three times in a lower voice, twice in a higher voice, three times in a lower voice, then twice in a higher voice?

AA: Um-hmm. Sometimes I can cut it short if I want to

You sing that verse three times, and you go up high twice, then you do it again three more times, go up high twice, then three more times, then after the last two you quit.

—Anthony Andreas

99

> I stayed in the service, because I would think everything was going to be the same when I came back, I would just fit back in. No way. When I came back, everybody was dead—gone—that knew anything.
>
> —*Alvino Siva*

cut it short and do it two times instead of three. It is up to the lead singer. The ones who sing with me know when I am going to do it. It is just automatic. They are just ready for it if I extend the music one more time.

AS: Yeah, and this is what the old people knew. See, Joe knew that. Oh heck, yes. Maybe I would have if the war hadn't come along. But I stayed in the service, because I would think everything was going to be the same when I came back, I would just fit back in. No way. When I came back, everybody was dead—gone—that knew anything.

DD: During the twenty years you were in the service, did you sing at all?

AS: Well, yes. When I was alone, I would sing and try to keep up remembering the songs.

DD: So how did you just start singing again after the war? Were there groups existing still?

AS: Joe was the only one. Joe Patencio was down here. This was another thing. When the last Patencio died, the older Patencio, which was Albert, they burnt the ceremonial house. This was the place where Joe would sing all night. He told me, "Now that my house is gone, I can't sing all night." So they would invite him, like they do me now, send him to Idyllwild, and maybe he would go sing for an hour, an hour and a half, two hours. I went with him to Soboba, down to Palm Springs. Then we would sing here at the fiesta. At the fiesta sometimes we would sing for three hours, maybe four hours. But we never did sing all night. I was just getting back into it when all of a sudden, Joe just died. He asked me, he used to say to me, "Come on down and stay with me for maybe a month and we will sing all these songs. Not only the bird songs, but the ceremonial songs." What we call our war dance songs. He knew those. He would say, "We will sing and we will record them together." I never had the chance to go.

DD: So what do you have to do to prepare for a bird singing engagement? If someone is going to have a party, they call you up and ask if you would come and sing? Do you get paid for this?

AA: No, I don't charge anything. In fact, I was told never

to charge. I could accept donations if people wanted to. Usually, people will feed me and my group. But I don't charge. If I am asked to sing—sometimes I go to the Colorado River and sing in Parker, Needles, Mojave—but they will give me some money. In fact, one time I sang and they gave me two packs of cigarettes. That meant more to me than the money because it was symbolic. The smokes, the cigarettes, were symbolic.

DD: So when the day of the singing comes, do you have a special outfit that you wear?

AA: No, we never did that.

DD: Then you travel light? You grab your rattle and go?

AA: Have rattle. Will travel. Yeah, I have been asked to sing at Summerton, Arizona for the Papagos—Yuma, Needles, Parker, and other places. Rincon, Pala, I sang there.

DD: How many people sing in your group?

AA: Well, right now there is sixteen of us. There is four male singers, four teenage boys, three teenage girls, and five under five years old.

DD: Do you meet regularly for practice?

AA: No. We only meet when we go to do a performance. I do a lot of performances, too, for non-Indian functions, for private parties, different functions. Historical functions. Like in Indio we did one. Now there, we dressed up. We have a costume for performing. The girls have a long dress. I wear a ribbon shirt and a cowboy hat. For lack of a costume, that's what we wear. The reason I wear a handkerchief around my neck is that I look at the old pictures and the men had their cowboy hat, or a hat of some sort, and a handkerchief around their neck. That's the closest I can identify with having any costume.

The girls, the dress they wear is similar to what the women wore in the early 1900s. The beadwork. Of course, it is fixed up more now, more colorful. But it is based on that. You will find that with other dance groups from other states. They all say that it is based on the costume worn in those days, but they just fixed it up. I'm sure that if the Indians had then what we have now, they would have used it.

DD: Your rattles are so beautiful! They look like they are one of a kind.

> I don't charge.... One time I sang and they gave me two packs of cigarettes. That meant more to me than the money because it was symbolic. The smokes, the cigarettes, were symbolic.
>
> —*Anthony Andreas*

If you harvest [the gourds]
too soon, then hang them up
to let them mature and
season, they don't get the
same sound as when you let it
ripen right on the vine.

—*Alvino Siva*

AS: I have a rattle here. This belonged to my father. It is cracked so I just keep it now. See the crack right there? Listen [shakes the rattle].

DD: Oh, it has a dull sound to it!

AS: This is what I use when I go perform [he shows a sky blue rattle]. I was going to put a design on that one, but I never did finish [shakes rattle].

DD: Wow. Beautiful, Alvino. I see you used some modern materials in construction, like acrylic paint and…

AS: [Laughs] Yeah. I should go out and gather some materials. See this little one here? I use this one when we do our ceremonial singing. This is the bottom half of a gourd, see? This one has a pretty good sound to it. I think that the reason was that it was vine-ripened, that makes a good sound. If you harvest it too soon, then hang them up to let them mature and season, they don't get the same sound as when you let it ripen right on the vine. So that is the main thing.

It grows all over the Southwest, in New Mexico. They are growing wild in Mexico. This was this fellow up in Anza that grew these. They are like melons.

AA: Yeah, it's a special gourd. There is only one kind. I don't know what the name is. Anyway, you get the gourd. You pick the one that has a good shape. It has to be round, because sometimes they lie flat on one side and get three-sided, or one side is flat. A good size is about four or five inches across.

I cut the neck off. I get a knife and clean out the inner part. Then I get a long screwdriver and clean out what is inside. I will get some pebbles and put in there. Then I boil it.

DD: What are the pebbles inside for?

AA: It holds it down, if it is boiling… It [boiling] helps— if it is kind of flat on one side, the water helps to puff it out a little bit. Maybe not all the way, but it helps. I boil it for an hour. Everyone does it differently. I know Alvino does it differently, and others too. I will take out the pebbles and let it dry out a couple of days out in the sun. Then I get it back, and by that time the inner part has loosened up. You can get a screwdriver and scrape around in there.

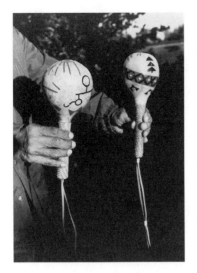 

That stuff in there dulls the sound. You have to get them all out. If I can't get them all out, I usually use broken glass and put it in there and shake it. There must be a better way than breaking glass. I don't know the way they did it in the old days. I used to get these little tacks at the hardware store, not thumbtacks, but little brads. I would put them in there and they would really clean it out real good.

AS: After I boil it [shakes rattle] and it softens that thing in there, then you can really scrape. But, you have to be careful because a lot of times you can get it too thin on one side or maybe the whole thing, and then it will just crack. So what I did with this to prevent that, I sprayed it with urethane. That is what I got on there [shakes rattle]. Modern Indian. They didn't have that years ago, so they had to be careful how they scraped it.

AA: Each gourd has a different tone. Sometimes you think you got a nice gourd, but when you get it finished, it's not a good sound. I have a few I play that have a good sound. I have others that are either too loud or too dull. The thickness of the gourd matters too. You put holes in it to get the sound to come out.

AS: And you can't tell how it is going to sound until it dries completely. On my other one, I was in a hurry to use it, so after I cleaned it out to where I thought it was thin enough, I put it in the oven to help dry it out. It came out pretty good.

Rattles by Alvino Siva

Photographs: Deborah Dozier

103

Years ago, they used the resin from the mesquite.... But I use modern methods. I went down to the hardware store and got some Elmer's glue and put it on there.

—*Alvino Siva*

AA: After that, I would get some seeds from the palm tree. I have to cure those. When you pick them, they have the fruit on them. I put the seeds in there without the handle, or I will get the handle and I kind of tape it and see if I need any more seeds. I play it a little bit [to hear] if it sounds just right, or I will take some seeds out. If I got the right amount of seeds in there, I will glue the handle on.

AS: The volume comes in the size. The bigger it is, the more [shakes rattle]. And then I found out, also, that what makes a lot of difference is the size of those little palm seeds. If you use the bigger seeds you will get a different sound altogether. I got a whole bunch of those seeds divided into the different sizes.

Then you get your little handle on there. Years ago, they used the resin from the mesquite. It is just like glue and [you] put it on there. But I use modern methods. I went down to the hardware store and got some Elmer's glue and put it on there [laughter].

AA: Well, if they had Elmer's glue in those days, they would use it. All of the tools I use are modern-day tools. I use it to make the holes, to shape it. I use a file, I use a knife.

One guy told me, "Hey, this is not an authentic Cahuilla gourd rattle." I said, "How come?" He said it was modern paint, it was acrylic and all that. I said, "Well, I am a Cahuilla Indian. I made that rattle, and if the Indians had this paint then, they would have used it." He said that I was right. He did say this isn't a traditional Cahuilla design. I told him that it was if I made it, because I am Cahuilla. It's like tamales or tacos, you know. Oh, that's Mexican food. Yeah, if a Mexican makes it. But if an Indian makes it, it's Indian food.

Then the handle is made out of cottonwood root, because it is lighter, easier to carve. But you can never tell. You have to find a cottonwood tree that has already fallen. So you have to go up the creek looking for one. Sometimes they are no good, they have worms. But you can't see it from the outside until you scrape it. It is a trial-and-error thing.

DD: Your handle looks different, Alvino.

AS: This one here, this is cedar, because cedar is light. Almost all of my rattle handles are made out of cedar. If you are going to shake it a long time, you want to have it light, see?

DD: So you put the handle on and then you paint it, varnish it?

AA: Then I paint it or varnish it.

DD: Do you have colors that you prefer or are there standard colors?

AA: I use any color I feel like using at the time.

AS: If you want to put designs, you can put designs on. But years ago, they didn't have no paintings. Only these modern Indians do all that stuff now.

Well, I am a Cahuilla Indian. I made that rattle, and if the Indians had this paint then, they would have used it.

—*Anthony Andreas*

Three gourds

These gourds will eventually become rattles if they make it through the long process of transformation; at any stage of the process the gourd may crack or be punctured by a slip of the hand, rendering it useless. Tending the gourds while they are still on the vine, turning and repositioning them regularly as they grow so that they do not flatten or dent, creates the proper round form.

Cleaning the gourd

The tough fibers which form the interior of the gourd must be removed. Failure to remove enough of the material results in a dulled sound which does not carry. This is perhaps the most tedious, time-consuming, and critical step of the process, and the step at which many gourds are ruptured and discarded.

The sound chamber is created by submerging the cleaned, weighted gourd in boiling water for an hour or so. This process softens any fibers remaining inside so they can be scraped away. The softening also permits the reforming of any portion of the rattle which is not perfectly round.

Carving the handle

Although the handle might seem like the least important part of the rattle, it connects the sound chambers of the rattles to the bodies of the singers, who must accompany the songs with rhythmic punctuation for many hours at a time with only a few short breaks. The handle must be well-balanced, light, porous, and comfortable to the touch to prevent fatigue in the singer's hands and arms. Cottonwood and cedar are preferred by many rattle makers.

Dates

These dates from the California fan palm, *Washingtonia filifera*, wait to be cleaned. The black, sugary flesh will be removed, the seeds will be allowed to dry, and the translucent, fibrous membrane which covers the seed will be rubbed off. The clean date pits are sorted by size and those with imperfections are discarded.

Finished bird song rattles

These three rattles, made by Anthony Andreas, combine acoustic excellence with perfect, modern form and artistic execution.

Photographs: Deborah Dozier

Hemet Maze Stone

There are maze petroglyphs throughout southern California, Baja California, and the Sonoran Desert region. Although no one alive remembers the meaning of this petroglyph, some Cahuilla believe it was made by a people who were here during the time the Cahuilla were gone on their migrations. Other Cahuilla believe these maze stones refer to their own migrations. This petroglyph, known as the Hemet Maze Stone, is considered the finest example of a maze stone in southern California. It is quite large; the boulder itself would fill an average living room. The maze is very deeply pecked into the surface; tiny grains of the rock are chipped away by repeatedly hitting it with a harder rock. The edges of the grooves have been smoothed.

Adapted from photo in the collection of the Southwest Museum, Los Angeles

ROCK ART

DEBORAH DOZIER: Do you remember the first time you saw any rock art as a child?

AA: Oh, the ones in Andreas Canyon. My grandmother showed me. She never went into detail about it, she just said it was here. I never asked her questions about it, it just stayed in my mind. I knew some of it was done for religious or some kind of ritual purposes, and others were done just for non-religious purposes. Just probably telling a story, or maybe a boundary marker, or a message. But most of it was, I think, religious markings. But you can't tell which is which. I think some was maybe lineage markings to let other people know this was our territory… I'm just guessing though. I was never told much about it, only that they were there.

JM: The only time that I have really ever talked about Cahuilla art within this boundary was with a Hopi. He goes and he looks for petroglyphs to read the boundaries and for the migration—as a Hopi, you know, the caretakers of the earth. He is always on alert to unite the tribes. To reinforce his belief of his world. I realized that we have petroglyphs and rock art, but it was never really explained to me who did it and why. The other day we were talking about boundaries, and we said, "Well, where is our section markers?" There should be section markers within the whole reservation.

I said that if there was really a boundary like that, our father or somebody would have said, "Here, here is this boundary and don't forget it. Here is where it's at, it's important that you know where it's at." That never was done. We started to laugh when we thought about it. What happened is when the surveyors came, there was a couple of Indians that found them and they ran them off. They never were allowed to survey the boundaries, so we never had sections marked within the

> Some [rock art] was done for religious or some kind of ritual purposes, and others were done just for non-religious purposes—just probably telling a story, or maybe a boundary marker, or a message. But most of it was, I think, religious markings.
> —*Anthony Andreas*

When [my dad] was having a problem, he went to this rock—this one power place—to try to find the solution.

—*JoMay Modesto*

reservation, just the outer boundary. Taking that feeling, is that what happened with the rock art? Was it something that belonged to other people? Maybe they were saying we would ignore it, because if we recognized it we would be acknowledging that maybe it was made by somebody before us or that we came into their territory, as a lot of people have speculated. Maybe they just chose not to deal with it. I know it is in places that are of religious significance to us.

DA: It is usually hidden in a difficult place to get to.

JM: Maybe we just weren't privy to the class of people that were allowed to know what it was and who it was.

DD: Did any of you every try and imitate or make your own rock art?

AA: No, when I grew up I did draw some on paper. Just for—to do something Cahuilla, I suppose.

DD: You said, though, that there is some modern-day rock art near your house?

JM: I don't think it is too modern because it must be at least, well, a thousand years ago. But it is in places. The one that I know of specifically, that I am familiar with, is in a sacred area. That whole area. My dad showed me where it was but he never told me what he thought it was for or who did it.

DD: Aren't there some modern names pecked in?

DA: In the moss, mostly. No, I guess it is in the rock too?

JM: Yeah, but mostly in the moss.

DA: "Florentina Lubo, 1916." I wonder why they wanted to do that. Aunt Flora has, my dad has, my uncle Sonny Leonard. You can go and see it etched into the rocks.

DD: By the old method of pecking with a rock hammer?

DA: I think some of it was the peck method. Aunt Flora's is. It is about this long [she stretches her arms as wide as she can]. It goes across the whole rock [laughs].

JM: I think maybe it was ownership, you were a part of it, you put your mark on it and maybe it was the Cahuilla thinking that you did have definite boundaries that you did establish yourself within. That you had the right to be able to put your mark on it.

I know my dad, when he was having a problem, he went to this rock, this one power place, to try to find the solution. He went specifically to this one place. I think maybe because, from what I know, it is in a sacred place, maybe that's what it was. But he said the wind blew. The wind would blow. There is different rocks that people would go to if they were having a problem or whatever.

DA: And this one isn't even on the reservation.

JM: So maybe that's what it was. It was kind of like lighting a candle in the church or, you know, you put your mark there. It was kind of like an offering or maybe it was, "This is me. Pray for me." A prayer request, a symbol—some kind of mark saying that you came and that it was there. A mark in your place in an unobtrusive way, because it was usually in a place where you couldn't see it. Usually in a very secretive place, a place of meditation. Most of them are in rocks—well of course, rock art [laughs]. But I mean in a cave within the rock.

That is probably what I would think of it as being. A place that you would go to. Most of the

Rock art tool kit

The tiny mortar and pestle pictured here were apparently never used to grind hematite ore into powder, but they illustrate the type of portable mortar and pestle used for the job. The pigment was carried in chunks like the ones shown here and ground to powder at the site where the painting would take place. The powder was either blown through a tube onto a surface painted with an oily binder or mixed with the fatty substance to form a kind of durable oil paint which was applied with a brush commonly made from plant fibers.

Photo from We Are Still Here *exhibition by Deborah Dozier*

> **To me, that is the way that you pray: you don't ask for it, but you ask for the ability to be able to handle it.**
>
> —*JoMay Modesto*

The rocks are alive, the rocks have power and you can use that, good or bad. You can use them as a source of power.

—*JoMay Modesto*

time, I think, those places were power places. That you sought the power, usually the power to handle something. To me, that is the way that you pray: you don't ask for it, but you ask for the ability to be able to handle it. How something was coming to you. And that's the reason I think that these places were for, that you asked for the ability to be able to do it. To be given the strength, the guidance, the insight—the insight to be able to deal with your problems.

So besides the religious and social and environmental, we also had another element, I think, that we haven't touched on. That is the psychology part to it. You know, that you have a place to go, instead of going to your analyst [laughs]. You were able to deal with it yourself. Like I said, the strength that you get from the earth and the rocks, all of those things. Like the hot water that we had, it is living water. The rocks are alive, the rocks have power, and you can use that, good or bad. You can use them as a source of power. The earth, everything. So psychologically, you know that if you go to that place and you ask for the strength and the power to be able to handle something, you have it, and you believe that you have it.

AS: Well, the rocks are what is pointing to us. Not only were they objects of power, but they were people at one time. Some have more powers than others. That they actually moved, they could do, you could talk to, and...

Maybe some of you don't know about the stories that were told to us [about] the guy that came and named a lot of the places. The old people used to say when he was making his movement, going through this area, they'd say the rocks and stuff was still hot when this man was making his movement. They said he sat down right here by Perris Lake, supposedly on the rock. They said he was a big man and they say that he left his prints of his penis and his testicles and his two little cheeks on this rock. They say it is still here. In fact, our sister that passed away, she saw it.

KS: She showed it to me, too.

AS: He was a powerful man. I guess he was one of the

demigods, and they had some more powerful ones. They trapped and they killed him.

KS: When he went on to the south, Parker [Arizona]. He died right below Julian [about ten miles south of Warner Hot Springs].

AS: But maybe it was just his time. But he knew that they were going to kill him. As he was, he could have known that what they were giving him was poison. See, they poisoned him. Anyway, when they got there, the night took him, so he made a little cup and they had this fire going. He knew that they already knew that he was coming, so they sent this red-tailed hawk to kill him. He knew that the hawk was coming, so he took a flat piece of rock and put it on his hip and sat by this fire. The hawk hit that rock, and killed itself.

He dressed the hawk and put it on this fire, and boy, they said it smelled so good. It was roasting, you could smell it and hear it. But he knew that if he would eat that, he would die. So he got his lance and stuck it through that bird and into the fire and a spring came up. He said, "Water that goes with that fire." And he moved on.

KS: Most of the people that knew and could understand rock art were probably gone by the 1850s or '60s. But some of the things I think passed on, like I asked my father about. I said, "Why did they mark all these, write all these things on the rocks?" He said some of them were done by the shamans wherever they met. It must have meant something to them for their power or something.

He said there were different marks, writings, some of them would indicate a water area to the people traveling on the trails. It would indicate to them where they could find food; some was left in rock shelters. Some told where you could hunt. Where deer would come and gather. And it was for when you go traveling. It told what you are supposed to do. He said that is the way it was for the Indian people.

They looked at that and knew what it meant at that time. He said all of us now can't interpret those because it is so far gone. You had to know and learn about it. But at the time I grew up the people who

> Not only were [the rocks] objects of power, but they were people at one time. Some have more powers than others...
>
> —*Alvino Siva*

Horse pictograph
This is a figure from a complex early 19th-century pictograph belived to represent the first interaction between Cahuilla people and Spaniards. Although no one knows for sure, the rider appears to be dressed in Spanish garb of the era of De Anza.

113

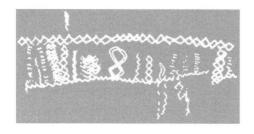

Pictograph

No one knows what these marks mean and no one knows who made them. Even the elders can only speculate. Is it a map, a boundary marker, a counting device, an events calendar?

Collection of Daniel McCarthy

knew were all gone. See, my dad was born in 1872. So that was gone already, the 1860s. So he just heard about it from the older people—what those signs were and why they were put there.

But what is it now? The thing we feel about it now is still there. When we go over to that area where they have those big boulders there, this side of Winchester, Twin Bluffs they call it, that's where the area is. When we first got there, Lowell [Bean] was there, and one archeologist. There was about seven of us, I think. When we got over there, I saw the markings, and you could see this giant boulder.

When I was standing over there, I was looking at all this and I had a feeling. A feeling that just came to me that it was a very, very sacred rock. That's probably where the shamans met and had to get their powers or to ask for it—whatever. I could feel it and I asked my brother if he felt it. He said, "Yes, I feel it." See, we both felt it. And I don't know if the others that were there felt that thing. I don't know, they never said anything.

Even later on, some of the older ones, older than my father was, they knew that those things were sacred. And they meant a lot to the people. We don't know anything about it now.

BASKETRY

KATHERINE SAUBEL: Oh gosh, basketry. It is old, old, old. They had to have some of them to carry their seeds and carry the acorns, and things like that. So they had that way back in ancient times. A lot of them made baskets; we have some here at the [Malki] museum now that are over one hundred years old. Some of them, I guess, close to two hundred. The baskets were used for cooking.

They didn't put the baskets on the fire [laughs]. They just put hot rocks in the water. Get that really boiling with the hot rocks and put your food in there. You would continue to put the hot rocks in there and cook it like that in the basket.

DD: Didn't your food get all full of ashes?

KS: No, no. Actually it is good for you. They didn't have it all soaking with ashes. You can heat a rock without putting a lot of ashes on it. Haven't you ever been a girl scout? [Laughter]

They were used for, like I said, for gathering different seeds and grain. Stuff like that. And also for storage and for cooking, for everything. For winnowing, they had winnowing baskets, they had cooking baskets, they had serving baskets, they had all different sizes and shapes.

DD: Gift baskets?

KS: Oh yes. That's when they got really fancy. When they had to give them to people as gifts. They would give them at a wedding. If someone died you offered them the baskets. Things like that.

> They were used for gathering different seeds and grain... and also for storage and for cooking.... They had winnowing baskets, they had cooking baskets, they had serving baskets, they had all different sizes and shapes.
>
> —*Katherine Saubel*

Cahuilla baskets from the Peabody Museum, Harvard University, photo N33837

115

Basketry

Basketry came back because art collectors wanted Cahuilla baskets, or other baskets. [The weavers] got paid for it, so they started making this into an art form—not to say it wasn't an art form before.

—*Anthony Andreas*

AA: Well, pottery and baskets were necessity items that had to be made. With the coming of the Europeans, they brought kettles and pots and pans, tin buckets. They stopped making those because it was easier to get a large can. I found a lot of that in the old village sites. With the bailing wire for handles. It was a long process to make these things. Our environment was changing. They started working on ranches. They started working on the railroads when it came through. We became farmers and ranchers ourselves. The whole system was changing.

DD: And if you dropped a tin can...

AA: Yeah, it wouldn't break like pottery. Basketry came back because art collectors wanted Cahuilla baskets, or other baskets. They got paid for it, so they started making this into an art form—not to say it wasn't an art form before. It was important in the early 1900s, 1920s. They started doing it for economic reasons.

DD: Did you have basket makers in your family?

AA: Both sides of my family, but my grandmother and her sisters and mother made baskets, some of these baskets I have here. I think my grandmother's sister made one for my grandmother. I don't remember which one it is. In the 1930s. It was a gift to my grandmother.

DD: Is there anyone in your family making baskets now?

AA: Not now.

DD: Anybody have an interest in relearning?

AA: There is always an interest, but it is just... A lot of this is something you just can't teach overnight. With the way we are living now, nine to five, have to go to work, they are busy raising families. You have to kind of grow up with it. I am not saying it can't be done, but you really have to sacrifice to learn a lot of this.

DD: Superhuman dedication seems to be required. And everybody in your family has to contribute to make it happen?

AA: Right. But it can be done. You just have to have the desire, like Donna Largo. She had the desire, so she has learned it. But then too, her mother was a basket maker. She was very close.

I know a lot of youngsters want to learn to make

Maria Los Angeles, 1899

Maria Los Angeles, working on a coiled basket. A bundle of deer grass rests in her lap. Like many Indian women of the time, she was forced to adapt to a cash economy; the money she was paid for her baskets allowed her to buy sugar, coffee, cloth, and other necessities.

Collection of the California Historical Society, Los Angeles, Department of Special Collections, University of Southern California Library

I finished one basket, a small one, that was just a plain one. I can't imagine my grandmother making the eagle design and the time she spent to get the dyes and to get it all together.

—*JoMay Modesto*

baskets, want to learn to do this. It is like learning the bird songs. They say they are going to bring their kids over so they can learn bird songs this weekend. Wait a minute. I have never taught anybody, and how are you going to learn in one weekend? That means I am just going to be a babysitter. If they really want to learn, they will come to where we are singing. That is how a lot of the kids... every time we sing, they were there. They grew up with it. My brother's boy, he was a little kid, he didn't know what he was doing. Now he is taller than us, and he is singing.

JM: My grandmother was a basket maker.

KS: Our mother was a basket maker, too.

JM: I found out how much ingenuity is required to make baskets and then how hard it is. I finished one basket, a small one, that was just a plain one. I can't imagine my grandmother making the eagle design and the time she spent to get the dyes and to get it all together.

Because of Donna Largo and Rosalie Valencia [1916–1995] doing contemporary baskets... it is still continuing. Like everything else, it is changing. It would be really effective if we could have some of these visitors trim down the thread—let them do it, so they could realize that it isn't easy to make something so beautiful out of something so simple.

DA: Baskets started off as a utility, but then became a form of an expression where a woman could really

Francisco Torres with mesquite granary, Torres-Martinez, c. 1917

Usually made by men, these granaries were woven of willow and rested on a mesquite or sycamore base elevated to discourage pests and to allow air circulation.

Collection of the California Historical Society, Los Angeles, Department of Special Collections, University of Southern California Library

Cahuilla baskets from the Peabody Museum, Harvard University, photo N33837

show her stuff: her patience, her colors, her designs, her capability, and her imagination. It became competitive. The tighter the weave, the finer the design, the prettier the colors—you know, it was a form of expression.

JM: I think that it was one of the best ways that they had to express themselves.

AA: And they could make some money. Today, we say it is terrible that they only were paid three or five dollars a basket, but in 1890 three or five dollars might have fed a family for a few weeks. It was good money.

JM: And then again, they tried to compete with each other as to who could make the finest, the most intricate basket. Cahuillas are very, very competitive, but it is so low key. You don't compete the same way that Western people do.

DA: You may even compete with yourself. You may be with a group, but you are competing against yourself.

JM: I think, probably, the designs and everything came more into play with [European] contact. People liked the baskets and so they valued them. This thing that was just a utility all of a sudden became a form of expression because it had a value and a desirability to be owned by somebody else. I guess it started off, probably, with baskets that were ceremonial. So more emphasis and more practice was put onto it. You had that form of a basket that was used as a tray basket, that had a purpose. But then you also had a ceremonial basket that you put a little bit more time and effort and beauty and design into.

119

Basketry

Gift baskets. The Spaniards and the American people that saw the baskets liked them. In their time women were really valued as basket makers. The prettier the design and stuff—it was a form of expression. When we were down there that last time and Lowell [Bean] had pictures of all those baskets, and the ones made by that one lady from White Water, you can tell when you see it that probably the same person made them. I know I can tell my grandmother's baskets. I can tell a Cahuilla basket.

DA: Oh, I saw the prettiest basket you would ever see, in Soboba. I happened to go into the house to talk with this young man. The basket was his wife's great-grandmother's. It is on the wall, but it looks like it is a painting, it is so good. A snake comes around like this and then goes like this [she motions in a spiral gesture]. It has a flat head and right here on the side there is a bunny rabbit that is perfect. I have never seen anything like it. It is just

Cahuilla baskets shown here are from the Peabody Museum, Harvard University, photos N33837 and N33838

perfect. It is like they drew it, instead of having a geometric pattern. It is the neatest basket I have ever seen. It is in what is called black and white. Well, this is like tans and blacks. I think it is black. I wanted to take a picture of it. I tried to get the daughter to put it in a museum on loan so that everybody could see it.

JM: You said it is almost like it is painted. That is hard to do that when you are working with the basket. The roundness got me.

I can tell Cahuilla baskets... not just by the designs, but by the colors. When you smell them... One thing I have never seen is a basket hat.

DD: Kathy and I saw lots of them in museum storage. A lot of them seemed to be a combination of half hat, half bread basket. Some were used to mold the shape of the mesquite cake, the mesquite bread. You could clearly see the food still encrusted in the interior.

DA: I wish we lived then. Life would be so much easier, because then everybody knew the rules [laughter].

I wish we lived then. Life would be so much easier, because then everybody knew the rules.

—*Dolores Alvarez*

Because of Donna Largo
and Rosalie Valencia
doing contemporary
baskets… it is still
continuing.

—*JoMay Modesto*

*Photographs: Deborah
Dozier*

Watching Donna Largo Make a Basket

As a child, Donna Largo learned about the basketry materials that grew on the Santa Rosa Reservation from her grandmother, but it was not until many years later that she learned to weave. As coordinator of the Hemet School District's Indian Education Program, she invited Elisa Mojada, the last weaver from Soboba Reservation, to teach basketry to children. As it turned out, Elisa Mojado showed her how to get started too, and in the years since then she has created many wonderful baskets and refined her skills. In recent years she has taught workshops in Cahuilla basketry and demonstrated the art at several museums.

Splitting the juncus

After the juncus reeds are pulled free of the rhizomes they are split, preferably before they begin to dry and harden. The base of the reed is split into three roughly equal sections. One section is held in each hand and the third section is held in the mouth; the top of the reed is held between the knees, and as even tension is applied the three sections are pulled apart. The result is three long strips ready for the next step. The juncus is frequently dried after this step of the process. The cardboard tube in the photo at left is filled with juncus withes.

Trimming and smoothing the withe

The next step is to refine the strips of juncus by removing the pithy white core of the reed and trimming the sides so that each withe is smooth and all are the same size: Mrs. Largo will keep the width of the reeds consistent for the entire basket. The pith is removed with a dull knife, as a sharp one would cut, rather than scrape, the fibers. The withe is pulled through a nail hole in a can lid (such as the one shown in the bottom photo) to trim the edges and produce a weaving strand of regular dimension with splinterless edges. Each woman prepares materials slightly differently, according to the traditions of her lineage and her personal taste. This is one element which produces an internal consistency in the body of work of each weaver.

Sorting the withes

After the withes have been properly smoothed and sized, they are sorted by color and coiled for convenience. The color of the plant will change as it dries. The red, basal ends of the reeds, and reeds dyed black by elderberry leaves and iron, are used for design elements. The golden upper portion of the reed is frequently used as a solid field of backdrop color or as negative space.

Many basket makers, Mrs. Largo among them, prefer to prepare each withe as it is used.

Harvesting and preparing materials is as much a part of the basket-making process as stitching a basket together, and often takes at least as much time.

Starting the basket

Finally, it is time for the most difficult step, making the basket "start." The start must be made with the most flexible materials, because the fibers must be able to coil in a spiral with a half-inch diameter without cracking or breaking. Any sharp angle created by a crack or break in the core bundle causes a disruption in the surface of the basket which can distort the finished form. Young basket makers were frequently given a basket start made for them by an elder relative to begin work upon, thereby saving them from the frustration of attempting a task nearly impossible for a novice.

Creating the core bundle

The core bundle of most Cahuilla baskets consists of the flower stalks, or culms, of *Muhlenbergia rigens,* commonly called deer grass. Mrs. Largo collects her deer grass in the fall after the seeds have matured and ripened but before the fall rains permit mildew damage. Once introduced into a basket, mildew will continue to be a problem, ultimately ruining the basket, and perhaps other baskets it contacts.

The end of the deer grass stalk where the flowers bloom is stripped of the needle-sharp flower and seed parts by rubbing it with a small piece of buckskin, which protects the basket maker's fingers from the splinters. Deer grass stems which are too large in diameter are cracked into lengthwise strips, compacting them to prevent future collapse of the bundle.

You can see the core of deer grass stalks projecting from the basket and more deer grass in the cardboard tube in the photo at right.

Inserting culms into the core bundle

It is very important for the basket maker to keep the diameter of each bundle consistent. If you look carefully at the basket in the photograph of Maria Los Angeles on page 115, you can see a string tied around the core bundle which extends outward from the basket coil. The string is a measuring gauge; new culms are added as the string around the core bundle slackens. Some contemporary women, including Mrs. Largo, use expended bullet casings with the ends sawed off; different caliber shells are used for different bundle diameters. Mrs. Largo prefers a 22-caliber shell.

Wrapping the core bundle

It is the process of wrapping the core bundle which adds pattern and additional structure to the basket. Red and black design elements decorated prehistoric and historic baskets. Mrs. Largo has added white, obtained from *Yucca whipplei,* to her palette of colors, using a technique shared with her by her Tohono O'odham friends. An awl is used to punch a small hole through the bundle, between the nearly parallel lines of the wrapping of the previous row. The sharpened end of a wet juncus withe is passed through the hole and pulled taut around the bundle. Another small hole is made between the next two nearly parallel lines, the end of the strand is again passed through and pulled tight. This process is repeated over and over again.

Determining pattern and form

Pattern design requires the basket weaver to predict the final outcome of a basket and the route to that outcome before the basket is even begun. If the basket surface is viewed as a circular, two-dimensional graph, the design can be viewed as units filled with color or left blank. The complexity of any design is thus limited only by the ability of the basket maker to manipulate the mathematics of stitch placement. The form of the basket is a matter of geometry. As each row of the coil is added, the angle of its placement, relative to the perpendicular axis of the basket, determines whether the walls of the basket flare or constrict or rise parallel to the axis. As with the pattern elements, these geometric calculations are accomplished without the use of any tools but the basket maker's heart, hands, and mind.

I am not saying it can't be done, but you really have to sacrifice to learn a lot of this.

—*Anthony Andreas*

Photographs: Deborah Dozier

125

Prehistoric ollas in cave shelter

Food and water were frequently stored in ceramic *ollas*. ["Olla" is the Spanish word for "pot," pronounced "oya."] Ollas were used in the house to keep water cool and food free of insects and rodents. In addition, they were portable, allowing the Cahuilla to extend their range of travel, not venturing too far without food and water.

Collection of Southwest Museum, Los Angeles

POTTERY

DOLORES ALVAREZ: I appreciate it. I appreciate it when you see a true artist, and mostly like the Pueblos. They put the designs, the birds. You don't see that in Cahuilla. Cahuillas were functional. I don't see it as really a form of art. I see it as more of a utility. Baskets were a little different than pottery. But pottery, every pot I have seen that was Cahuilla was very functional.

JM: Basically, ceramic pots are pretty crude. Even the consistency of the clay wasn't really very practiced, no emphasis is put on it. It was just a utensil.

DD: Did any of your forbears make pottery, that you know of?

DA: Aunt Flora did. She knew where the clay deposits were and she would get it. I remember she had one nice big one. It stood about this high [she indicates about three feet] and stood in the back room on the top of the closet. Daddy made some once. He seemed to enjoy it.

JM: I tried it just to see if I could do it. It was kind of fun polishing it with the stone and all of that.

KS: The only pottery makers here in southern California were the Diegueños and the Cahuilla. The Diegueños were first. I think the beginning of it was not here at all. We traded with the Mojaves. We got that from there over to here. That was a long, long time before [European] contact when they were made here. But they didn't have it here before the Mojaves traded it. But when they learned from the Mojave, then we made it. My paternal grandmother was a pottery maker.

I asked my father about that. I said, "How did they make that? I want to do it when I get old." He said I better start learning now. And he told me how it was prepared, how the clay was prepared, how you did it. Oh, everything like that. I said, "Maybe one of these days I will try it."

I asked my father about [pottery]. I said, "How did they make that? I want to do it when I get old." He said I better start learning now.

—*Katherine Saubel*

DD: Where did the clay come from?

KS: It comes from special areas. I know they have one over here, because my husband's grandmother got it from the hills back here.

DD: In Morongo?

KS: Uh-huh. And she was a pottery maker, his grandmother. There is supposed to be another area where they get pottery. It depends on where you get it. [Some] are red clay, like, and the other's a kind of brownish clay. They are back here. And then up in my area, where my grandmother got it, they had that up there, too. So in different areas, they used all that.

DD: How did they construct pots?

KS: I was asking my father about that. I said, "Well, how do you begin with that?" "Well," he said, "you get clay and dry it and grind it. Then you sift it and when you get all that fine, then you add something like gravel but a little thinner, they put that in. That holds that together," he said. And then you could put in some, like grass, and that holds it together. And when you burn it after you fix it, that all blends together and your pot holds together. I have often wondered about that because the Cahuilla pottery is so thin. Have you ever looked at it? How can they hold instead of cracking?

DD: So then what did they do? Get it all fine and mix it?

KS: Yes, and then they put it all together like you do dough or something. Then you get it all working. He said the old women used to do it on their knees. Then you get that, and you put coils around and around. Then you get the rock, it's a really slick rock, and the paddle. They use that for the inside. With the rock and the paddle you work it. You work it along as you go by. He said, "The bigger you want it, the bigger coil you make. The smaller you want, the smaller they are." That's what he said, and I said I would try it one of these days, if I feel like it. I won't let anybody know [laughs].

DD: Where did the pots go, why did they stop making and using them?

KS: Well, I believe they stopped, probably in the 1900s I guess. My grandmother died in the 1920s—'24, I think. All of those people that were making them were dying. I don't think the young ones took over. Maybe some of them did, I don't know. But I know, in my case, we didn't.

DD: What did they do without pots, though?

KS: Well, that was just when the white man came in with his pots and pans—and frying pans. We all "went to pot" with the lard and things like that. When the Indians first lived here, in earlier times, there was never a fat Indian. They walked, they hunted. The women gathered, they walked a long ways. They were all slim, all the time [laughs]. When the white man introduced the frying pan and the lard, there goes our shape.

The Cahuilla pottery is so thin. Have you ever looked at it? How can they hold instead of cracking?

—*Katherine Saubel*

129

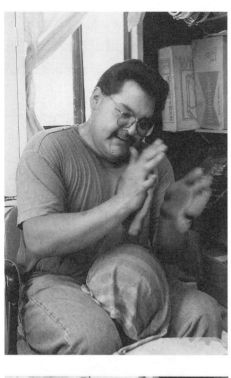

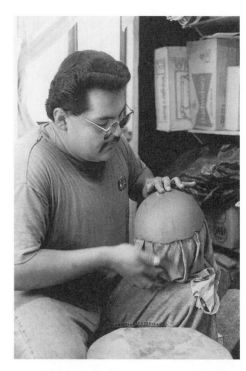

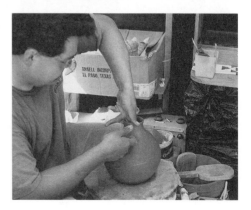

David Largo's Pottery

David Largo, a young man from Santa Rosa Reservation (Donna Largo's son), is the leading Cahuilla pottery maker. He began making pottery in his twenties after working in silver and leather for many years. When he discovered pottery it was as if his hands knew what to do, and within a few years he had advanced his art to a mature level not practiced by any Cahuilla for more than seventy years. Thanks to him many young Cahuilla people are now interested in making ollas.

The first step is to dig the clay. Then it is dried and ground into a fine powder in the same way corn is ground, on a flat metate (slab) with a mano (hand-sized stone). The powder is mixed with water, finely ground pottery pieces, and a little ground vegetal material, called temper, until the desired consistency is reached.

The prepared, plastic clay is ready to be formed around the bottom of another pot to form a shallow bowl. Ropes of clay are added to the rim of the bowl until the desired final size is reached. As in a basket, the position of the coils determines if the pot wall slants in or out or rises straight up. The clay must be kept evenly damp, but not wet, during this procedure, not a simple task in a land where the humidity frequently hovers below ten percent.

The coils are pressed and smoothed together to form a solid surface. A smooth, flat, small, round stone is held against the inside of the pot while it is slapped on the outside with a paddle made of wood or palm. This process compacts the clay, forming a stronger vessel, and evens out any small deformity of shape.

The outside is polished with a very smooth, round stone to create the final surface.

The olla is allowed to dry slowly; fast drying would cause it to crack. Finally, the vessels which make it this far are painted and fired in an earthen oven. The arrangement of pots and fuel in the oven determines where flashes of red and black color will remain as the oxygen content of the oven changes.

Malki Museum Billboard, c. 1972

Since 1966, the Malki Museum's major public event has
been its annual barbeque fiesta. This fiesta draws thousands of visitors to Malki each year—many of whom are
visiting an Indian reservation for the first time—but
Indian guests are the heart of the fiesta. Many remain all
night long around the blazing central campfire, singing
the songs and dancing the dances that otherwise would
rapidly pass out of knowledge.

Collection of the Malki Museum

WE ARE STILL HERE

KATHERINE SAUBEL: When the first Spaniards landed in the territory, the Indian people were looking at them and were afraid of them. They thought they were ghosts. They thought the Spanish were dead people because they looked so white; they needed blood, they were dying people. Here they were, the conquerors, you know, they were coming in and the Cahuilla didn't want to go near them because they thought they had some kind of disease, see? That's what the Indians said when they were looking at them. But it wasn't that way at all. The Spanish were here to get what they were going to get from us—and they did.

The Cahuilla were afraid of them. Not only then but after a while because of the way they were treated. They were pushed out of their land and they were afraid. They didn't have no rights in their own land. They lost everything. I think that was just the beginning of the end of my people.

And then after a while some Cahuillas tried to learn the Spanish language and they did go to work for a lot of Spaniards that had the big ranches here. They went to work for them, either to take care of their cows and horses, like cowboys, or to work their fields, whatever jobs they could get. Some of them had to go from their traditional homes to shear the lambs at the times when they had to be sheared. They got jobs like that. Any job they could get. That's what they did afterwards.

And then after the Spanish, the Mexicans came. The Mexicans were kind of a little bit lenient to the Indian because they, the Mexicans, were Indian too. The Spanish conquered them and so they had a little bit of compassion for the Indian and tried to give some portions of land—not little portions, but big portions—to the Indian people. But before the Mexicans completed the giving, the Anglos took over.

> They thought the Spanish were dead people because they looked so white.... Here they were, the conquerors... and the Cahuilla didn't want to go near them because they thought they had some kind of disease.
>
> —*Katherine Saubel*

133

A Cahuilla labor camp near Riverside, 1886

This is Big Springs Rancheria, perched on the side of Little Rubidoux Mountain, on the west bank of the Santa Ana River, on the outskirts of Riverside. This town had become a migrant camp which supplied workers to meet the day labor needs of Riverside families and businesses. The houses are made of cane, which still grows abundantly in the marshy areas of the Santa Ana riverbed.

Collection of the City of Riverside, Historical Resources Department

They were just as bad as the Spanish. They were just there to destroy the Indians.

That's when we really became, you might say, beggars, because we had no place to hunt, no place to gather anymore. We were just held down to the different areas. Sometimes to areas where we didn't even belong—we were moved around by whoever was in power. It was really a trauma for my people. They became so, how would you say... They were always hungry now, they were always in a sad situation. I guess they just had to live with what little they could get just to survive. But they were really destroyed.

When they [the Americans] came, we Cahuilla were really just ignored for quite, I think, a long time. In fact, they just wanted to clear us off the area. I think that's why most of the time, my people, the Cahuillas, were afraid to go anywhere. They were safer in their own areas. Those were in the interior part, and I think that's why we are still here today—on account of that geographic situation. Otherwise, we would have been like the coastal Indians. They were destroyed right away. Their culture was ruined. Like the Chumash, the Gabrielinos, and all that.

DD: Was it the American government that took the Cupeños out of Warner Springs?

KS: I don't really understand that at all. I know that when the Indians were going to be taken off their land... the Americans said that area was being given to Jack Warner. One of the Spanish land grants went to him. The Indians never knew anything about Spanish land grants. They knew it was their land, they were living there. But the Americans had already given that land to Warner without the knowledge of the Indian people. And when they came to remove them, they just removed them by force.

DD: What did they do?

KS: My father was telling me—he was there, and this is what he saw. When they came there he said they just brought this long band of wagons, and they just threw the Indians' belongings in there, and I guess just actually put the people on there by force. And a lot of the people were crying. Everybody was

> That's when we really became, you might say, beggars, because we had no place to hunt, no place to gather anymore.
> —*Katherine Saubel*

Ramona Lubo, c. 1890

In 1882, at the request of the United States government, Helen Hunt Jackson was contracted to survey the Indians of southern California and to determine where land suitable for reservations was located. It was then she heard the story of Ramona Lubo (seen in this picture), a young Cahuilla woman, and her husband, Juan Diego. A white man, Sam Temple, unjustly accused Juan Diego of stealing his horse and then shot and killed him. Jackson said in an 1883 letter to friends, "I am going to write a novel, in which will be set forth some Indian experiences in a way to move people's hearts." Her novel is remembered in the annual Ramona Pageant held in Hemet, California.

Photograph: Professor May
Collection of Southwest Museum, Los Angeles

The village of Cupa at Warner's Hot Springs, 1903

This photograph shows Warner's Hot Springs before the Cupeño people were forced from the land. You can see Indian adobe and brush dwellings as well as a church and clapboard houses.

Photograph: Charles F. Lummis
Collection of Southwest Museum, Los Angeles

> They just brought this long band of wagons, and they just threw the Indians' belongings in there, and I guess just actually put the people on there by force.
>
> —*Katherine Saubel*

crying. A lot of the old people ran off into the hills. A lot of them were never seen again.

DD: Where were they taking them on these wagons?

KS: They had to take them from Warner Springs to Pala. They had to go by the road that goes out to Temecula and then turns left into Pala. And that's quite a ways. I don't know how long it took them, but it probably had to take them maybe a day, two days, or three days to get over there.

DD: Why were they taking them there?

KS: That's one of the things too. The Indians had their own boundary lines, and the people at Warner's were taken into the Luiseños' territory. And a lot of those Indians from Warner's didn't want to go there because it was not their area. But the white man didn't care about that, didn't care that they had their own areas where they lived. So they forced them over there to live with the Luiseños. I heard the Luiseños were very offended because the Americans didn't tell them anything over there either, they just walked them in there. Because they were Indians, they didn't care where they put them. But the Indian is not that way. He has his own villages, his own areas. That was disruptive when they were moved.

137

The council that tried to prevent the eviction

This group met with the Commissioner of Indian Affairs on March 17, 1902 to try to prevent the eviction of the Cupeño people from Cupa. Some of these leaders would later join and become active in the Mission Indian Federation.

Photograph: Charles F. Lummis
Collection of Southwest Museum, Los Angeles

Exiles of Cupa, 1903

"They just brought this long band of wagons, and they just threw the Indians' belongings in there, and I guess just actually put the people on there by force... Everybody was crying. A lot of the old people ran off into the hills. A lot of them were never seen again."

—*Katherine Saubel*

Photo: Charles F. Lummis Collection of Southwest Museum, Los Angeles

Cattle herds en route to Pala, 1902

Men herd cattle along the road during the Cupeño relocation to Pala.

Photograph: Sawyer Collection of Southwest Museum, Los Angeles

The wagon train en route to Pala, May 12-14, 1903

"They had to go by the road that goes out to Temecula and then turns left into Pala. And that's quite a ways."

—*Katherine Saubel*

Photo: Charles F. Lummis Collection of Southwest Museum, Los Angeles

Issuing rations, 1903

Rations were issued at Pauba Ranch, the site of the second night's camp. Cahuilla people and many other Native Americans remember occasions when unscrupulous Indian agents sold their ancestors the rations that had been sent to satisfy the terms of treaty agreements.

Photograph: Sawyer Collection of Southwest Museum, Los Angeles

They had food here, they had wild berries, they had acorns, they had things that they could use. They had lots of game here. The antelopes were still here. The bighorns, the deer, the rabbit.... And then when the Anglos came, they lost all that and they got hungry.

—Katherine Saubel

DD: Tell me about the smallpox epidemics.

KS: It's really one of the things that destroyed the Cahuilla people, I believe. I think at that time, smallpox was introduced to the Cahuilla people deliberately. They wanted to get rid of us. They deliberately sent those blankets and things like that infected with smallpox to the Indian people. At that time, when the Cahuillas got that disease, almost seventy percent maybe, more or less, died out because they didn't know about the disease. That's what killed them off. That just really reduced us—besides going hungry and not having our own areas anymore. We were really, really devastated by the small pox.

DD: What's the implication of having seventy percent of your population gone?

KS: Well, to me... When I asked my father that, I said, "The white man said we were about 5,000 or whatever, 6,000 here." He said, "No, there were more than that. He said at that time there were about 15,000. The way he said it, it was about 15,000. Maybe more, he said, because we were so widespread, [it was] a long territory that the Cahuilla lived in. There was a lot of people at one time. Each village had one or two hundred people. There was a lot of villages. There must have been that much, that's what he said.

DD: What happens to your social structure, your religious structure, your economic structure, when seventy percent of your people are gone?

KS: We really lost all of our economic way of things that we had here. Before contact, my father said every person never went hungry. They had food here, they had wild berries, they had acorns, they had things that they could use. They had lots of game here. The antelopes were still here. The bighorns, the deer, the rabbit. And so he said we always had food. And then when the Anglos came, they lost all that and they got hungry. In a lot of pictures you will see now where they look so ragged and everything else. That's on account of that. Everything was destroyed and they couldn't use this or that. I think that's the time when some of them, I believe, would just give up.

What really surprised me was when they made the treaties with the Indians here at that time, in the 1850s, and they promised so many things that they were supposed to give them—large parcels of land where they could live, not just like five acres like they have now. I think it was supposed to be 160 acres, or so many acres to the families. But that never happened. Of course, those treaties were never ratified by the Congress, so the Indians never got the land that was given to them. Finally, in the late, I think, 1880s or '90s, they set aside the reservations. The Indians used to live up there where the town is now. On the side there [indicating a 270° arc] and over here. They were moved over here, all around here. The land they were moved from was taken over years ago. And who could they appeal to? They didn't have no voice anywhere. The Indians couldn't say anything against the white man. He had all the rights. The Indian had nothing. So they just went down and lost everything.

DD: Fifty years ago Perfecto Segundo, a venerated shaman, predicted the end of Cahuilla culture as it was.* Do you think there will be a Cahuilla culture five hundred years from now?

KS: I doubt it. I doubt it very much. Because in the first place, the Cahuilla is terminating itself even from being Cahuilla, by intermarriage. I think that is one of the things that is going to take away from who we are, especially the Cahuilla. From the beginning, the Cahuilla people always followed the father's line. And now, if the father is not Cahuilla, where is the line? There will be other Indians, I suppose, in five hundred years, but I don't think there will be any Cahuilla.

> There will be other Indians, I suppose, in five hundred years, but I don't think there will be any Cahuilla.
>
> —*Katherine Saubel*

---

* In the early 1930s Perfecto Segundo's said, "There was a lot of Indian people here at one time. There is no more. No place is theirs anymore in these effigy ceremonies. There is no longer any other dances, ceremonial dances. There is no eagle dance. Nothing is there anymore. Now that is gone. That is all.

"The kids, the children that are left now will never know what it was. This is the way it will be, this is the way it is. It is finished. It is already done. It is understood. We do not know what it will be now. Everything is disappearing. I am the one that is talking now, Perfecto Segundo. I am 74 years old. That is why I am saying this."

The land is the most important thing you can think of. Without that, you are nothing.

—*Katherine Saubel*

And that is if we live that long. If we are not poisoned out. All of us, not just Cahuillas. Well, I think the only way we can do that now is to train the children. The children, I think, are the ones that can grow up to be who they are... if we instruct them in the right way. I think they can still retain some part of it when they get older. Otherwise, without them, we are going to be gone.

DD: How do you feel about the culture disappearing?

KS: Well, I feel bad about it, because it is happening now in my lifetime. I have seen a lot of changes. I have rode in the wagons a long time ago before I knew the car. I never knew the car until I moved to Palm Springs. All these things that we used a long time ago, from that time on up to the cars, and then when I found out about the trains, and about the airplanes and everything else—it is just going, going, going. There are more different changes now, like to outer space. We are the ones that are really going to be gone. The ones that lived on this continent. The first inhabitants.

DD: What do we lose if Indian culture disappears?

KS: The worst thing I worry about is the land itself. The white man is destroying himself with all his nuclear powers and this and that. Look at how many people are fighting against the nuclear things over here in the Nevada desert. It is going to be all over pretty soon. It will probably be all over. And things like that, the people... this is not going to be just right here, it will be all over the world. Look at that Chernobyl, at whatever happened there. It is still going through killing a lot of people. Even into Sweden and all those places. It is just not in that one area, it goes all over. We may not be here in five hundred years, the way things are going.

Indian culture, I think, was the only way to live with the respect of everything around you. Respect yourself and the people. Really get along, try to live in peace, and to preserve this land. The land is the most important thing you can think of. Without that, you are nothing.

DD: What is being done to preserve Cahuilla culture?

KS: I read that book on Palm Springs that Francisco Patencio wrote [*Stories and Legends of the Palm*

Cahuilla School, 1903

Cahuilla Indian children attended the Colorado Desert School in Martinez. The building was made of plastered adobe. The unhappy expressions on the children's faces may be due to the length of time the children had to stand for the photograph, and the midmorning heat of the summer day. The construction project underway gives testimony to the fierce nature of the heat: a shade roof is being added to the building. Other schools, like St. Boniface School in Banning, were run by Catholic missionaries.

Collection of the California Historical Society, Los Angeles, Department of Special Collections, University of Southern California Library

Graduating class, Sherman Indian School, 1905
Many Indian children from northern, central, and southern California were forced off their reservations into
boarding schools run by the American government,
whose "progressive" idea was to acculturate these children into a life of servitude by teaching the girls to cook,
style hair, sew, and bake, while the boys were taught
agriculture, saddle making, and carpentry. Few if any
went on to college. This is the graduating class of 1905.
We know from the roll books that at least two of the
students who graduated that year were Pass Cahuilla.
These schools had an unexpected effect: social and political affiliations formed at Indian schools lasted a lifetime and led to intertribal marriages and the formation
of the Mission Indian Federation and other political
lobbying groups.
Collection of the Sherman Indian School Museum

Springs Indians]. In the front part he said this was written for the children that are to come because they won't know anymore. I think that is important to talk about. But we have to explain a lot of it. We have to explain who we are and where we are coming from. It encompasses all of those things, to show exactly where we are at, so they realize and appreciate, and to get the ideas across that we want to show them—all kinds of things. But if they don't understand where we are coming from, it is pointless.

DA: I think that a lot of it has to do with the work that Lowell [Bean] has done and the people that he has worked with, to bring that awareness back. They said we were "digger" Indians. It was like you were animals. You dug here, you dug there. Then I found out that we owned property. We own property here, we own property there. We had our own roads. I learned all this from what they said. There was a purpose for it all, it wasn't just because you were going to own and acquire, the materialist kind of stuff. It wasn't that at all.

What I can see is men, it would have been the men, sitting around and discussing how something was going to work. The things that you did, like disposing of your fingernails and your hair. That was all ecology, to keep things clean. Everything that they thought about was for a reason and a purpose. I find it really fascinating that they thought that far ahead, like playing chess. These intelligent people had a system that worked out far better than what the Plains had.

JM: Well, I think a long time ago—even, let's say, with my grandmother—that the culture changed. They had to change from the beads to money, the shell money, and then it went to contemporary money. When we went to using the material, everything was replaced.

Change has always been something that Cahuillas have had to do to survive. To accept that… to change and to constantly go figure out, "How much do I give, how do I really want to share?" You change, you end up doing it because that means survival of the people.

> We have to explain who we are and where we are coming from… so they realize and appreciate, and to get the ideas across that we want to show them. But if they don't understand where we are coming from, it is pointless.
>
> —*Katherine Saubel*

Mission Indian Federation, 1930

Founded to establish a base of political power, the federation was composed of leaders from the numerous tribes of central and southern California, a deliberate move which resulted in a united Indian front, resisting subjugation through political organization.

This photograph was taken at the home of Jonathan Tibbet, an Anglo-American dedicated to helping Indian people claim their civil rights. The Mission Indian Federation frequently congregated at his home in Riverside between 1910 and 1940.

Photograph: E. N. Fairchild
Collection of the Riverside Municipal Museum

Mission Indian Federation newspaper

The Mission Indian Federation published a newspaper as a means of informing the white population of southern California about the conditions under which the Mission Indians fought for survival. It ran stories about issues affecting Indian people and about the activities of the federation, as well as news from various reservations, a valuable service during an era when the rural nature of the reservations precluded easy communication among communities.

Collection of National Archives, Pacific Southwest Region

DA: I think it had a lot of effect on their self-esteem when men had to go out to work and make a living for their families because the land wasn't there to be used. They may have been that powerful person, important person, in their clan and with their family. And then when they get out and they are working for this white, rich farmer it was going to be racial and degrading, and I think that is why a lot of them started drinking. They couldn't handle it. The woman, being still in the house, was protected from having to get out there.

DD: How did the Malki Museum get started?

KS: Jane Penn started that. She had left here when she was a young girl, a teenager, in fact. She must have been about 16 or 17. She went to live in Los Angeles. She worked and lived in Los Angeles. Then she came home when she was 49 years old. When she came back she realized that all the people that lived here were gone, the older people. She just had her cousin and her aunt living. She talked to her cousin, saying that they had given her some artifacts of theirs, her cousin. She said she should start something to save all this. She said there was nobody around anymore and we should have something. She spoke to Lowell Bean, and he is the one who helped her to get all of us together and we started that museum. On a shoestring—we didn't have any money at all. That was in 1963. There was a lot of them that helped us out that were non-Indians.

The Malki Museum is one of the nice things that happened to the Indian people, because that is

Malki Museum, c. 1970

Malki is the Cahuilla name for the place where Morongo
Reservation is today, hence the name Malki Museum.
Founded in 1963 by Mrs. Jane Penn, Lowell Bean, Harry
Lawton, Mariano and Katherine Saubel, and others, the
Malki was the first all-Indian museum on a southern
California Indian reservation. Under the direction of
president Katherine Saubel, the Malki Museum has
served to promote Cahuilla culture since it opened its
doors. The Malki Museum Press, solely owned by the
Malki Museum publishes the *Journal of California and
Great Basin Anthropology*. Its distinguished editorial
board has also directed the publication of many books
on southern California Indian culture. In addition, the
Malki Museum grants many community college scholar-
ships for southern California Indian students and main-
tains an ethnobotanic garden.

Collection of the Malki Museum

holding things there that was just the remnants of what we used to be, what the Cahuilla culture was in the past. That is the only place where the Indian fifty or sixty years from now can find out who they were, what language they spoke. Everything is there. I think it is just like a library or something for the Indian. Not only the Indian, but the non-Indian that wants to learn about us. We have had a lot of scholars working there with us to find out about different things. I think it is something that really helps the people understand who was here and what they had done.

DD: Tell me about the Malki Museum Press.

KS: We realized that a lot of things were being lost. We also realized that the books that were written about the Cahuilla, or about any Indian for that matter, were written by non-Indians. It was never from our point of view, it was from theirs all the time. At Malki Press, a lot of Indian authors speak as Indian people. So I think that is one of the things that is really interesting to me. That we can do that, you know, have our own press.

We have some Indian authors published by Malki Press that put down their own recollections... like when I was about 12 or 13 years old, when I spoke Cahuilla to my peers, my own people that went to school with me, they would answer me in English all the time. I talked to them in my language. That's when I realized that the language is going to go right away, because they don't want to talk it. They understood every bit of it, they could speak it at that time, but they were no longer using it. That is why I worked on the dictionary of our language.

Then I realized, too, that the plants and things we used, what our people were doctored with, that was disappearing. That's why I helped to write this book *[Temalpakh]* about the plants. Because I know that nobody else is going to use them. I knew a lot of this from my mother's side. That's why I started to keep a notebook, when I was in high school, of the plants and things like that. When I met Dr. Bean, I showed him that notebook. I said, "Can we do something about this?" He said, "Yes, we will work

The Malki Museum is one of the nice things that happened to the Indian people.... That is the only place where the Indian fifty or sixty years from now can find out who they were, what language they spoke.

—*Katherine Saubel*

Even if they don't know the language, at least they will know the history.... They would have that sense of pride.

—*Anthony Andreas*

on it. I will supply all the Latin names and you will supply the Indian names." With his help I worked on that book. I thought that was one of the best things that we did.

DD: How many volumes has the Malki Press published?

KS: We have already published about maybe 32 or 33 different books. We have one on the line right now, the medicine book of the Chumash people.* After that, we have another book to publish. That will be a big book with a lot of pictures. This is the Tongva or Gabrielino book.**

DD: Now the Agua Caliente Band has plans to construct a cultural center/museum in Palm Springs?

AA: Yes. We hope it will be open in 1995.*** It will be a museum of Agua Caliente history and an archive for bird song recordings. It will also have a space where we put up temporary exhibitions about other Indians. We have worked with many different people to plan the most modern museum possible. We hope to be accredited by the American Association of Museums. You have to be a really good museum to do that.

It is one way we can save the bird songs. I don't know if the younger generations will know the bird songs completely. That's another reason we are trying to build this museum in Palm Springs. To have things that our younger kids can learn from and see, because we are not close anymore. We are so separated. That is nobody's fault. That is just the way things are, the way things happen. And this museum would bring everybody together to know their history. Even if they don't know the language, at least they will know the history, and "This is my great-grandfather, my great-grandmother. These songs, so-and-so sang them, that is my great-uncle." They would have that sense of pride. It will make them proud, even if they don't talk the language or sing the songs. That history part is very important.

DD: What are the challenges facing the Cahuilla as the culture moves into the future?

* *Chumash Healing,* by Philip L. Walker and Travis Hudson, published in 1993.
** *The First Angelinos,* by William McCawley, published in 1996.
*** The Agua Caliente Cultural Center in Palm Springs, now open.

150

KS: Years ago the non-Indian came in here. Since then we have always had the problem. I call it the White problem, but everybody else calls it the Indian problem. It is not that. We never had a problem here until the non-Indian got here, then we had problems. So it is not the Indian problem as far as the Indian is concerned [laughs].

I don't know what will be. The only thing I want is for them to leave us alone so we can live in peace. We don't bother anybody. But it just doesn't seem that way. Too many unscrupulous developers. Too many of them are greedy people, and that's what is destroying us—greed.

I hope our message goes through, that what we are doing will open up the eyes of the public to what's happening, what is going on today. The federal government is trying to allow the people to put toxic wastes in the reservations. When you are trying to preserve your way of life, your culture and everything, trying to save what little you have, if you don't have any more land, what are you going to do? Nothing. See, there is no more. That is the ending of it.

I think there is a purpose to all of this. From the beginning, there was genocide, like smallpox, and then killing the Indians in central California by poisoning them, and things like that. But we were so strong, we just hung on. We're *here*. But that's the whole purpose—to get rid of us, as you know. I never read it in history books, but the idea of the President, Andrew Jackson, was to annihilate us from the face of the earth—to kill us, hunt us like animals. Each head $50 or $5, whatever. That's the whole thing.

They find all different ways to do that—the Allotment Act, the Termination Act, all these different acts. They were not going to help the Indians. They are going to destroy us.

But it is still going on, like I said. Now they are still continuing genocide at the present time with the toxic waste and garbage things on our reservations. And that is going to destroy us, because it is going to destroy the land, the water, the air, everything around us.

> I call it the White problem, but everybody else calls it the Indian problem.
>
> —*Katherine Saubel*

They are still continuing genocide at the present time with the toxic waste and garbage [dumps] on our reservations.

—*Katherine Saubel*

JM: Protecting the land is really hard. Even with the rock art, if we were to protect everything, we would have to protect from the desert to wherever our territory was. No matter what you are into, you are going to find something, some artifact, something. There is always a turmoil, all the time—what to do with it.

DA: There are a lot of caves where there are spearheads or flints and prehistoric animals in this area, southern California. A lot of those areas are where Indians probably lived. The evidence they are finding now is just recent, two to three thousand years.

We found an arrowhead when we were doing our tribal hall. The archeological report said it was six thousand years old. It was on top of the ground. They were just walking across and found it. They sent that one to Washington for dating. They sent it back to us. It was kind of sad, because here is this person who just sent it off. We didn't even know it was gone. When it came back it was kind of weird. We opened the package up at the tribal hall during a meeting and here it had gone so far and been away so long. But they gave it back and we did what we wanted to do with it. We reburied it.

When we did something, it was taken care of at that time. Six thousand years later, we have to deal with this arrowhead that we had. We chose to rebury it. We don't know how to do the ceremonies anymore. The ceremonies protect us. If we don't do it right, then it will come back to us. You are always in a conflict with yourself and the reality of what you are dealing with. It is really difficult to have to go through all of these things.

KS: So when an arrowhead or rock art is found, what are we going to do with it? We don't know who made those. Whatever the power in those rocks, it is still there. Whether it will hurt us if we touch it and we take it to our home or we take it to a museum we don't know, because we don't have the shamans anymore. They are the ones that know.

We may have the shamans. Their is power probably came to them and talked to them, but it talked to them in Indian and they didn't understand what the power was saying. This is the problem now.

You are born with the power. It comes to you very young. And it may come to you when you are older, but you have to recognize it. You have to be an Indian to recognize it. If you are an Indian in just name, you don't understand what he is saying. So you just ignore it, so it either leaves you or it is there, but you don't know what to do with it.

I guess that is why my brother Cruz said, "We are lost. Nobody knows, we might as well forget it." But, you cannot forget it. You are an Indian, and whatever is going to affect you is not going to say, "Well, you don't speak Indian anymore so I won't bother you." He says, "You are an Indian, and I am going to kill you." And that is what they will do.

So you can't forget it. I don't know how much Indian you have to have in you before it leaves—how much other blood besides Indian—before it leaves you—but if you are Indian, it is there for you.

You are born with the power. It comes to you very young. And it may come to you when you are older, but you have to recognize it.

—Katherine Saubel

Bibliography

Amos, Ajato. *The Use of Oral Tradition for Reconstructing the Past,* 8th International Congress of Anthropological and Ethnological Sciences. Tokyo: Science Council of Japan, 3:368-370, 1968.

Aschmann, Homer. *The Evolution of a Wild Landscape and its Persistence in Southern California.* Annals of the Association of American Geographers, 49(3)2:34-57, 1959.

Ball, Edward K. *Early Uses of California Plants,* California Natural History Guide 10. Berkeley: University of California Press, 1965.

Barrows, David Prescott. *The Ethnobotany of the Cahuilla Indians of Southern California.* University of Chicago Press, 1900.

Baumhoff, Martin A. *Ecological Determinants of Aboriginal California Populations.* University of California Publications in American Archaeology and Ethnology 49(2):155-236, 1963.

Bean, Lowell J. "Cultural Change in Cahuilla Religious and Political Leadership Patterns" in *Cultural Change and Stability: Essays in Memory of Olive Ruth Barker and George C. Barker,* edited by R. L. Beals. Berkeley: Department of Anthropology, University of California, 1-10, 1964.

—— *Mukat's People: The Cahuilla Indians of Southern California.* Berkeley: University of California Press, 1972.

—— and Lisa J. Bourgeault. *The Cahuilla.* New York: Chelsea House Publishers, 1989.

—— and Katherine Siva Saubel. *Temalpakh (From the Earth): Cahuilla Indian Knowledge and Usage of Plants.* Morongo Indian Reservation, CA: Malki Museum Press, 1972.

——, Sylvia Brakke Vane and Jackson Young. *The Cahuilla Landscape: The Santa Rosa and San Jacinto Mountains.* Menlo Park, CA: Ballena Press, 1991.

—— and Harry Lawton. *The Cahuilla Indians of Southern California.* Morongo Indian Reservation, CA: Malki Museum Press, 1965.

Beattie, George W. "San Bernardino Valley Before the Americans Came." *California Historical Quarterly* 12:111-124, 1933.

Beidler, Peter G. and Kathleen Molohon. *Fig Tree John: An Indian in Fact and Fiction.* Tucson: University of Arizona Press, 1977.

Blackburn, Thomas C. and Travis Hudson. *Time's Flotsam: Overseas Collections of California Indian Material Culture.* Menlo Park, CA: Ballena Press and Santa Barbara Museum of Natural History, 1990.

Bolton, Herbert E., ed. *Anza's California Expeditions,* Vol. 1-5. Berkeley: University of California Press, 1930.

Bibliography

Brasher, Janet G. "Relationships Between the Desert Cahuilla Indians and the Honey Mesquite." *Michigan Academician* 5(3):385-396, 1973.

Brumgardt, John R. and Larry L. Bowles. *People of the Magic Waters: The Cahuilla Indians of Palm Springs*. Palm Springs, CA: Etc Publications, 1981.

Byers, John R., Jr. "The Matter of Helen Hunt Jackson's Ramona: From Fact to Fiction." *American Indian Quarterly* 2(4):331-346, 1975.

Carniero, Robert. "Cultural Adaptation," in *International Encyclopedia of the Social Sciences,* edited by David L. Sills 3:551-554. New York: Macmillan and the Free Press, 1968.

Caughey, John W., ed. *The Indians of Southern California in 1852*. The B. D. Wilson Report. The Selection of Contemporary Comment. San Marino, CA: The Huntington Library, 1952.

Cline, Lora L. *Just Before Sunset*. Jacumba, CA: J & L Enterprises, 1984.

Corle, Edwin. *Fig Tree John*. New York: Liveright Publishing Corp, 1935.

Drucker, Philip. *Culture Element Distributions: Southern California*. Anthropological Records, Berkeley and Los Angeles: University of California Publications, 1:1-52, 1937.

Fenenga, Gerrit L. and Eric M. Fisher, "The Cahuilla Use of Piyatem, Larvae of the White-lined Sphinx Moth (*Hyles lineata*) as Food." *Journal of California Anthropology* 5(1):84-89, 1978.

Forbes, Jack D. *Native Americans of California and Nevada*. Healdsburg, CA: Naturegraph Publishers, 1969.

Frazer, Robert W. "Lovell's Report on the Cahuilla Indians, 1854." *Journal of San Diego History* 22(1):4-10, 1976.

Garces, Francisco. *Record of Travels in Arizona and California in 1775-1776*. New translation by John Galvin. San Francisco: John Howell Books, 1965.

Garr, Daniel J. "Power and Priorities: Church-State Boundary Disputes in California." *California History* 57(4):364-375, 1978.

Gifford, Edward W. *Clans and Moieties in Southern California*. University of California Publications in American Archaeology and Ethnology 14:155-219, 1918.

—— *California Kinship Terminologies*. University of California Publications in American Archaeology and Ethnology 18:1-285, 1922.

Grinnell, J. and H. S. Swartz. *Birds and Mammals of the San Jacinto Mountains*. University of California Publications in Zoology 10:178-397, 1908.

Hahn, Henry. "Music of the Early North American West." *Pacific Historian* 15(1):25-38, 1971.

Hall, H. M. *A Botanical Survey of the San Jacinto Mountains*. University of California Publications in Botany 1:1-140, 1902.

Harvey, H. R. "Population of the Cahuilla Indians: Decline and its Causes." *Eugenics Quarterly* 14(3):185-198, 1967.

Hayes, Benjamin. *Pioneer Notes from the Diaries of Judge Benjamin Hayes*. Privately printed, Los Angeles, 1929.

Hedges, Ken. *Shamanistic Aspects of California Rock Art*. San Diego: San Diego Museum of Man, N.D.

——— The Rock Art of Andreas Canyon. For Cultural Systems Research, Inc., 1985.

Heintzelman, S. P. Report on Southern California Indians. In 34th Congress, 3rd Session, House Executive Document 76, Serial 906:34-58. Washington, D.C.: Government Printing Office, 1857.

Heizer, Robert F. "California Earthquakes of the Mission Period of 1769-1838." *California Journal of Mines and Geology,* Report No. 37 of the State Mineralogist: 219-224, 1941.

——— *The Eighteen Unratified Treaties of 1851-1852 Between the California Indians and the United States Government.* Archaeological Research Facility, Berkeley: University of California, 1972.

——— An Early Cahuilla Ethnographic Sketch. *Masterkey* 48(1):14-21., 1974.

———, ed. *The Destruction of California Indians.* Santa Barbara, CA: Peregrine Smith Inc., 1974.

——— *They Were Only Diggers: A Collection of Articles from California Newspapers, 1851-1866, on Indian and White Relations.* Ramona, CA: Ballena Press, 1974.

——— and Albert B. Elasser. *The Natural World of the California Indians.* Berkeley: University of California Press, 1980.

Hooper, Lucile. *The Cahuilla Indians.* University of California Publications in American Archaeology and Ethnology 16:316-379, 1920.

Hughes, Tom. "History of Banning and San Gorgonio Pass." *Banning Record,* 1938.

Hutchinson, C. Alan. "The Mexican Government and the Mission Indians of Upper California, 1821-1835." *The Americas* 21(4):335-362, 1964.

James, Harry C. *The Cahuilla Indians.* Morongo Indian Reservation, CA: Malki Museum Press, 1969. Reprint of Los Angeles: Westernlore Press, 1960.

Johnson, William A. *Through the Years with William A. Johnson: A Family Album.* Riverside, CA: privately published, 1955.

Johnston, Francis J. *The Bradshaw Trail: Narrative and Notes.* Riverside, CA: Historical Commission Press, 1977.

Kennedy, Don H. "Ramona's People." *Californians* 4(5):46-49, 1986.

Kroeber, A. L. *Shoshonean Dialects of California.* University of California Publications in American Archaeology and Ethnology 4:65-165, 1907.

——— *Basket Designs of the Mission Indians.* Anthropological Papers of the American Museum of Natural History 20:149-183, 1922.

——— *Handbook of the Indians of California.* Smithsonian Institute Bureau of American Ethnology Bulletin 78:1-995, 1925.

——— and Lucile Hooper. *Studies in Cahuilla Culture.* Morongo Indian Reservation, CA: Malki Museum Press, 1978.

Langenwalter, Rebecca E. "A Possible Shaman's Cache from Ca-Riv-102, Hemet, California." *Journal of California and Great Basin Anthropology* 1(2):233-244, 1980.

Bibliography

Lando, Richard and Ruby E. Modesto. "Temal Wakhish: a Desert Cahuilla Village." *Journal of California Anthropology* 4(1):95-112, 1977.

Lawton, Harry and Lowell Bean. "A Preliminary Reconstruction of Aboriginal Agricultural Technology Among the Cahuilla." *The Indian Historian* 1(5):18-24, 29, 1968.

Mathes, Valerie Sherer. "Helen Hunt Jackson: Official Agent to the California Mission Indians." *Southern California Quarterly* 63(1):63-82, 1981.

McConnell, Virginia. "'H.H,' Colorado, and the Indian Problem." *Journal of the West* 12(2):272-280, 1973.

Meighan, Clement W. "Indians and California Missions." *Southern California Quarterly* 69(3):187-201, 1987.

Modesto, Ruby and Guy Mount. *Not for Innocent Ears*. Angelus Oaks, CA: Sweetlight Books, 1980.

O'Neal, Lulu Rasmussen. *A Peculiar Piece of the Desert: The Story of California's Morongo Basin*. Los Angeles: Westernlore Press, 1957.

Oswalt, Wendell H. "The Cahuilla Gatherers in the Desert." In *This Land Was Theirs—a Study of the North American Indian*. New York: John W. Wiley, 141-184, 1966.

Patencio, Francisco. *Stories and Legends of the Palm Springs Indians as Told to Margaret Boynton*. Los Angeles: Times Mirror Press, 1943.

Phillips, George H. *Chiefs and Challengers: Indian Resistance and Cooperation in Southern California*. Berkeley: University of California Press, 1975.

Quimby, Garfield M. *History of the Potrero Ranch and its Neighbors*. Fresno, CA: California History Books, 1975.

Rawls, James J. *The Indians of California*. Norman, OK: University of Oklahoma Press, 1984.

Ritter, Lawrence S. "Chief Meyers [1909-17]." In *The Glory of Their Times: The Story of the Early Days of Baseball Told by the Men Who Played It*. New York: The Macmillan Company, 162-176, 1966.

Ryan, R. Mark. *Mammals of Deep Canyon*. Palm Springs, CA: Palm Springs Desert Museum, 1968.

Sahlins, Marshall. "The Segmentary Lineage: An Organization of Predatory Expansion." *American Anthropologist* 63:332-345, 1961.

Saubel, Katherine Siva and Anne Galloway. *I'isniyatam (Designs): A Cahuilla Word Book*. Morongo Indian Reservation, CA: Malki Museum Press, 1977.

———— and Pamela Munro. *Chem'ivillu'*. Los Angeles: American Indian Studies Center, University of California, 1981.

Shipek, Florence C. "Mission Indians and Indians of California Land Claims." *American Indian Quarterly* 13(4):409-420, 1989.

Smith, Gerald A. and Wilson G. Turner. *Indian Rock Art of Southern California with Selected Petroglyph Catalog*. San Bernardino, CA: San Bernardino County Museum Association, 1975.

Steward, Julian H. *Petroglyphs of California and Adjoining States*. University of California Publications in American Archaeology and Ethnology 24:47-238, 1926.

Strong, William Duncan. *Aboriginal Society in Southern California*. Berkeley: University of California Press, 1929.

Sutton, Imre. "Land Tenure and Changing Occupations on Indian Reservations in Southern California." Doctoral dissertation in Geography on file at the University of California, Los Angeles, 1964.

Thomas, Richard M. "The Mission Indians: A Study of Leadership and Cultural Change." Doctoral dissertation in Anthropology on file at the University of California, Los Angeles, 1964.

Treganza, Adan E. "The 'Ancient Stone Fish Traps' of the Coachella Valley, Southern California." *American Antiquity* 10(3):285-294, 1945.

Turner, Justin G. "The First Letter from Palm Springs: The Jose Romero Story." *Southern California Quarterly* 56(2):123-134, 1974.

Voght, Martha. "Shamans and Padres: the Religion of the Southern California Mission Indians." *Pacific Historical Review* 36(4):363-373, 1967.

Waterman, Thomas T. "Analysis of the Mission Indian Creation." *American Anthropologist* 11(1):41-45, 1909.

Weinland, John. Unpublished Correspondence to and from Rev. John Weinland, Moravian Missionary to the Morongo Reservation. San Marino, CA: Huntington Library, N.D.

Wilke, Philip J. "Late Prehistoric Human Ecology at Lake Cahuilla, Coachella Valley, California." Doctoral dissertation in Anthropology on file at the University of California, Riverside, 1976.

Williamson, Lt. R. S. Report of Explorations in California for Railroad Routes to Connect with Routes near the 35th and 32nd Parallels of North Latitude, Vol 5. Washington, D.C.: Beverly Tucker, 1856.

Zigmund, Maurice. "Ethnobotanical Studies Among California and Great Basin Shoshonean." Unpublished doctoral dissertation on file at Yale University, 1941.